MW01627458

Jeanne S. Chall, Ph.D. • Helen M. Popp, Ed.D.

Acknowledgements

Grateful acknowledgement is made to the following for permission to reprint the copyrighted material listed below:

Page 21: "Sometimes" from I FEEL THE SAME WAY by Lilian Moore. Copyright © 1967, 1995 by Lilian Moore. Used by permission of Marian Reiner for the author.

Page 89: "Chums" from THE LAUGHING MUSE by Arthur Guiterman. Reprinted by permission of Louise H. Sclove.

Page 115: "Jump or Jiggle" by Evelyn Beyer, from ANOTHER HERE AND NOW STORY BOOK by Lucy Sprague Mitchell, copyright 1937 by E. P. Dutton, renewed © 1965 by Lucy Sprague Mitchell. Used by permission of Dutton Children's Books, a division of Penguin Putnam Inc.

Page 167: "Sun After Rain" from SMALL WONDERS by Norma Farber, copyright © 1964, 1968, 1975, 1976, 1978, 1979 by Norma Farber. Used by permission of Coward-McCann, Inc., a division of Penguin Putnam Inc.

Every effort has been made to trace the ownership of all copyrighted material and to secure the necessary permissions to reprint these selections. In the event of any question arising as to the use of any material, the editor and the publisher express regret for any inadvertent error and will make the necessary correction in future printings.

Illustrations: Harry Norcross, Devon Chaney, Rob Williams, Murray Callahan, Laurie Conley

Photographs: Fine Line Photography, Inc., 4, 7, 10, 14, 16, 21, 31, 36, 50, 55, 64, 70, 72, 81, 84,106, 121, 138, 158, 167, 177; Ellen B. Senisi, 145; all others, Photo Disc, Inc.

ISBN 978-0-8454-3480-2
© 2007 The Continental Press, Inc.

No part of this publication may be reproduced in any form or by any means, electronic, mechanical, photocopying, recording, or otherwise, without the prior written permission of the publisher. All rights reserved. Printed in the United States of America.

Table of Contents

Level B

Unit 1 Theme: Look and Listen

Auditory and Visual Discrimination

Unit 2 Theme: Playtime

Consonants **s, m, t, b, f, r** Short Vowels **a, i**

Unit 3 Theme: In and Out

Consonants **n, p, d, h, c, g** Short Vowels **o, e**

Unit 4

Theme: Pets

Consonants **j, l, k, v, w, z, qu, y** Short Vowel **u**

Unit 5

Theme: Jump Up, Jump Down

Consonant Blends and Digraphs; Plurals; Compound and Two-syllable Words

Unit 6

Theme: At the Park

Long Vowels **a, i, o, u**; Inflectional Endings

Unit 7

Theme: Rainy Days, Sunny Days

Long Vowel Digraphs; Y as a Vowel; Contractions

Unit 1

STOP-GO

Automobiles

In

a

row

Wait to go
While the signal says:

STOP

Red light's gone!
Green light's on!
Horns blow!
And the row
Starts

to

GO

Dorothy Baruch

Dear Family,

As part of our reading program this year, we are using the **Chall-Popp Phonics** program. Your child will be learning phonics—letters and the sounds they stand for. Phonics teaches children how to "decode" printed words (sometimes this is called "sounding out").

Children know many words before they read—words they hear and use every day. As they learn to decode print, they will read many of these familiar words and recognize them.

We will start out by learning about rhymes and reviewing the letters of the alphabet. We will also learn some common sight words, words like "the" and "what." These are the first steps in phonics instruction.

You can help your child get ready to learn phonics and to read.

- Read to your child often—stories and poems especially.
- As you read a poem, such as the one on the other side of this page, pause at the end of a line and let your child say the rhyming word.
- Encourage your child to notice letters on things around the house—boxes and magazines, for example. Name the letters and have your child point to each letter you name.

Reading together and playing with sounds and letters will be fun for you and your child. We hope you will enjoy helping your child learn to read.

Name

Name the pictures in each box.
Circle the two pictures in each box whose names rhyme.

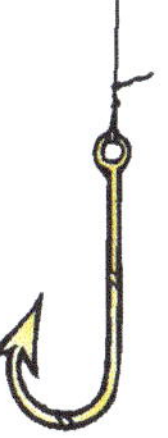

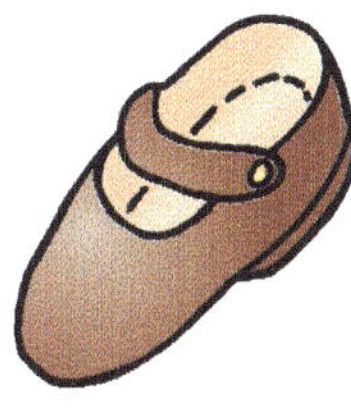

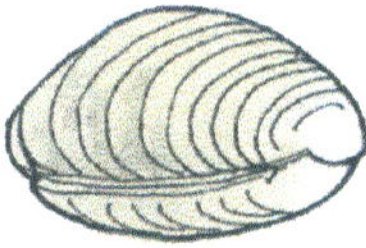

© Continental Press

Name the pictures.
Draw lines to match pictures whose names rhyme.

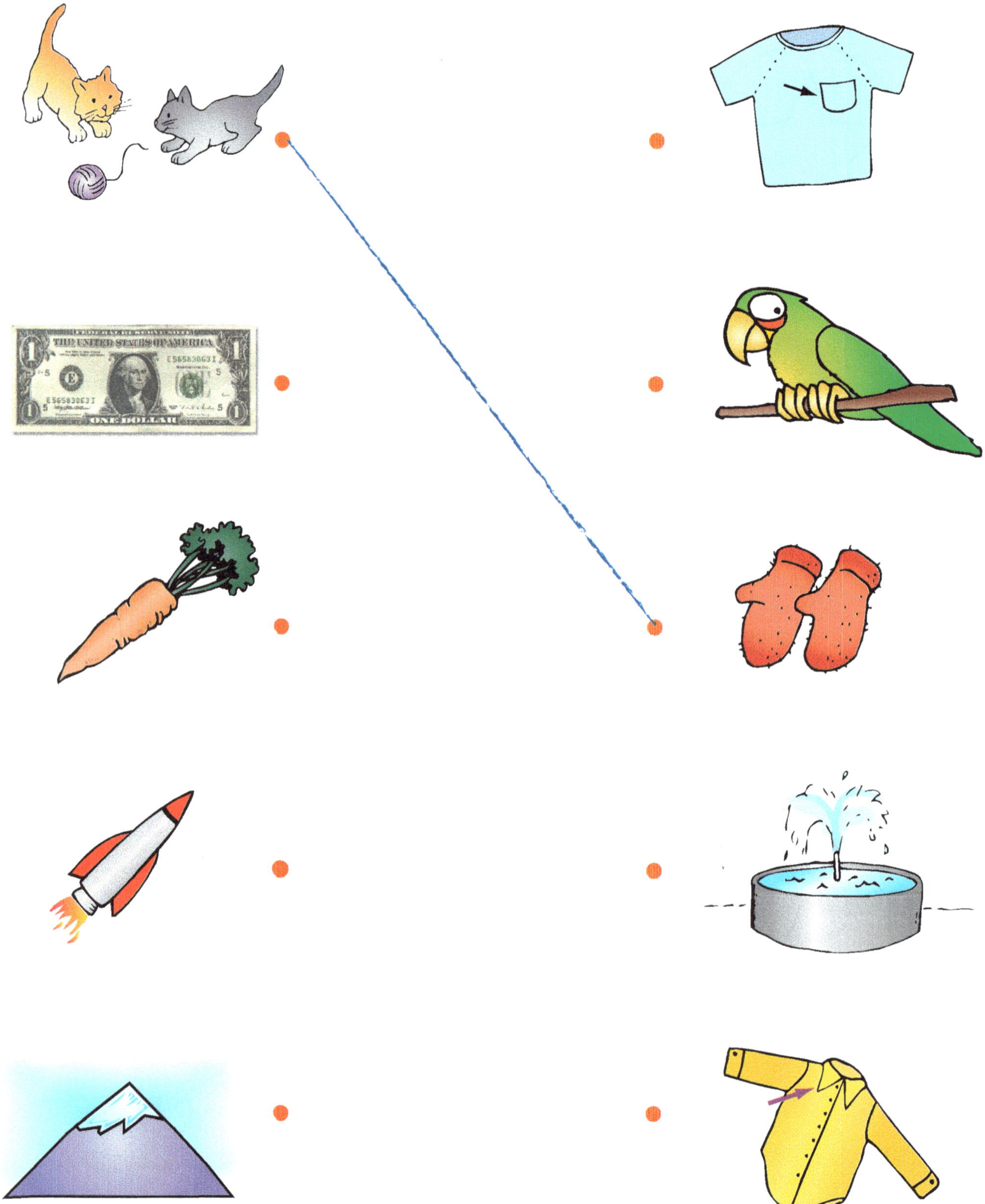

Name

ABCDEFG are capital letters.
abcdefg are lowercase letters.

Draw a path from each capital letter to its lowercase letter.

© Continental Press

Connect the dots in alphabetical order. Start with A at the ★.

ABCDEFGHIJKLMNOPQRSTUVWXYZ

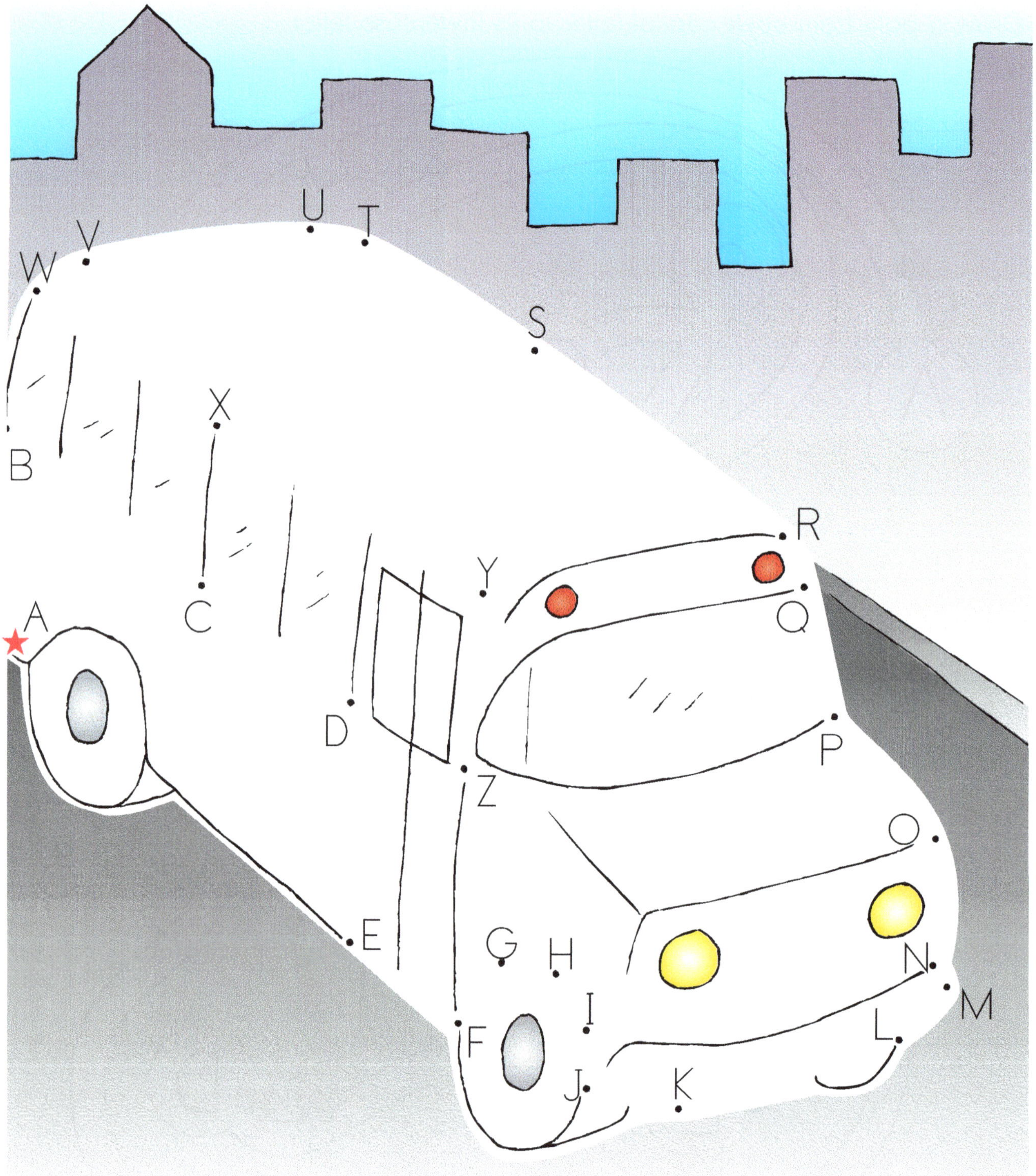

Name

HIJKLM are capital letters.
hijklm are lowercase letters.

Draw a circle around the matching capital and lowercase letters in each box.

1	2	3	4
F h H l	L j i I	I j g J	k K H f

5	6	7	8
L d H l	h M m K	K h H l	i I L j

9	10	11	12
I g j J	k M h K	k L I l	K h m M

© Continental Press

Connect the dots in alphabetical order. Start with a at the ★.

a b c d e f g h i j k l m n o p q r s t u v w x y z

Name

NOPQRST are capital letters.

nopqrst are lowercase letters.

Draw a path from each capital letter to its lowercase letter.

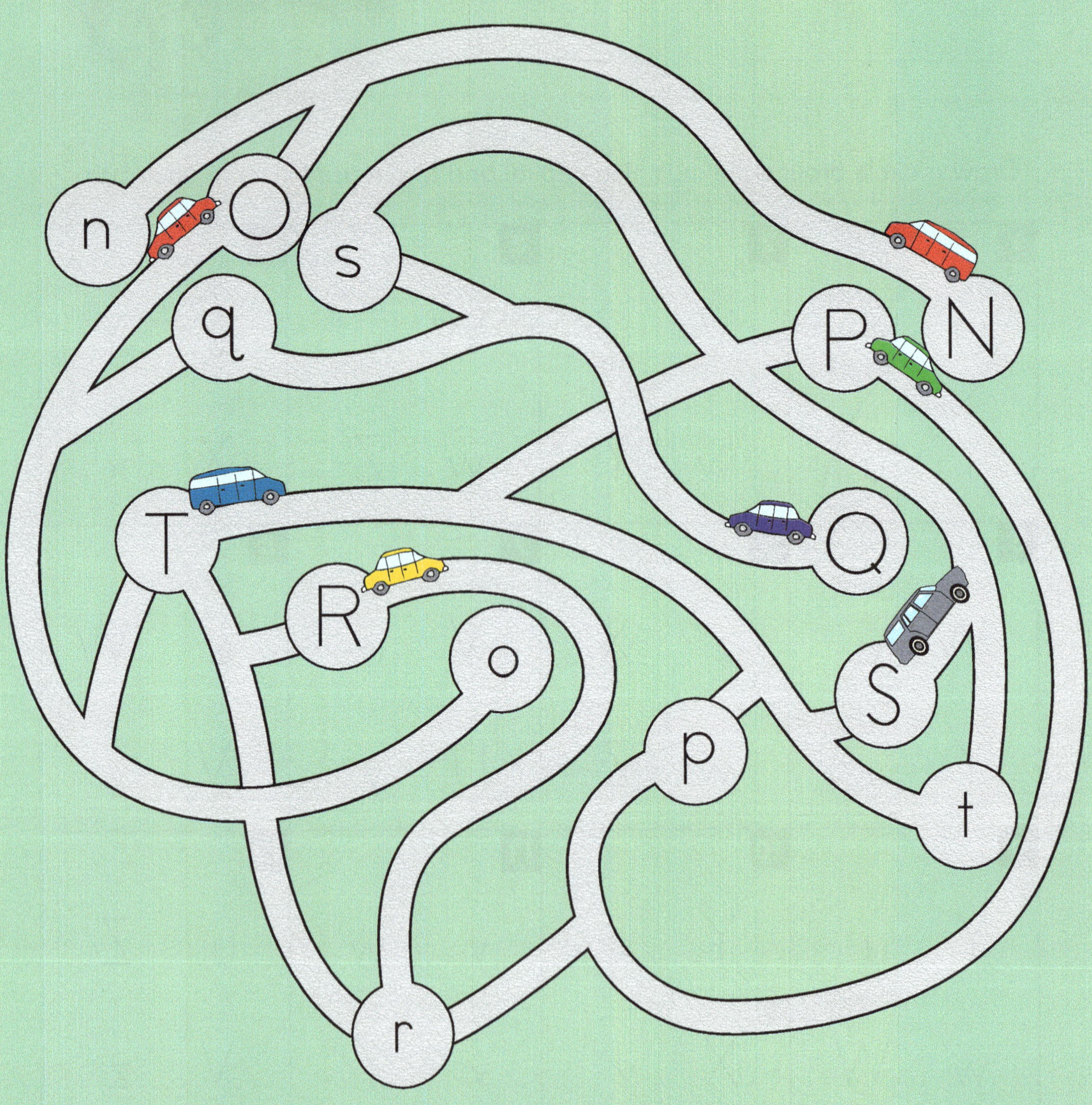

© Continental Press

U V W X Y Z are capital letters.
u v w x y z are lowercase letters.

Draw a circle around the matching capital and lowercase letters in each box.

1	2	3	4
U v Y u	V v w Y	W v w Z	v Y X x
5	**6**	**7**	**8**
W y Y v	z X w Z	V u U y	u W V v
9	**10**	**11**	**12**
Y u w W	Y x X v	y w v Y	u Z V z

Name

Name the letters in each row as you trace them.
Then print each letter on the line below.

A B C D E F G

A

H I J K L M N

H

O P Q R S T

O

Name the letters in each row as you trace them.
Then print each letter on the line below.

U V W X Y Z

U

a b c d e f g

a

h i j k l m n

h

Name

Name the letters in each row as you trace them.
Then print each letter on the line below.

o p q r s t

o

u v w x y z

u

Trace the capital letters in the word **ALPHABET**.
Then print the word **alphabet** in lowercase letters.

ALPHABET

a

© Continental Press

Name the letter over each traffic light.
Circle each word inside the light that begins with that letter.

Name ____________________

Circle the words in each row that are the same as the first word.

the	the	then	the	they
has	had	has	has	his
said	said	sad	say	said
to	to	to	it	at
get	go	get	get	got
for	for	far	from	for
me	my	me	men	me
good	good	gone	good	goes

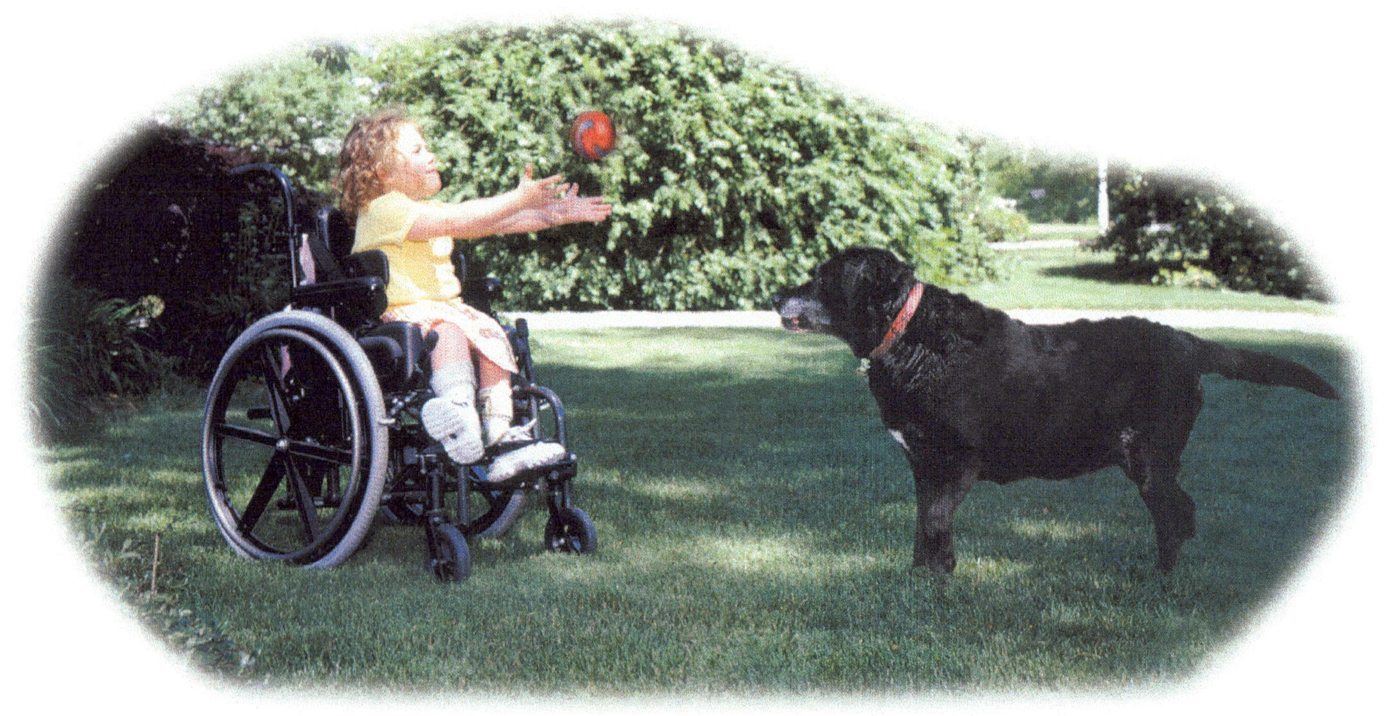

The [girl] has a [ball].

The [girl] said to the [dog],

"Get the [ball] for me."

The [dog] has the [ball].

"Good [dog],"

said the [girl].

cut

fold

© Continental Press

4
YIELD

2
SCHOOL BUS
STOP

5
ONE WAY

7

Name

Listen to the word your teacher says.
Circle the picture in the box whose name rhymes with the word.

Print the missing capital or lowercase letters in alphabetical order.

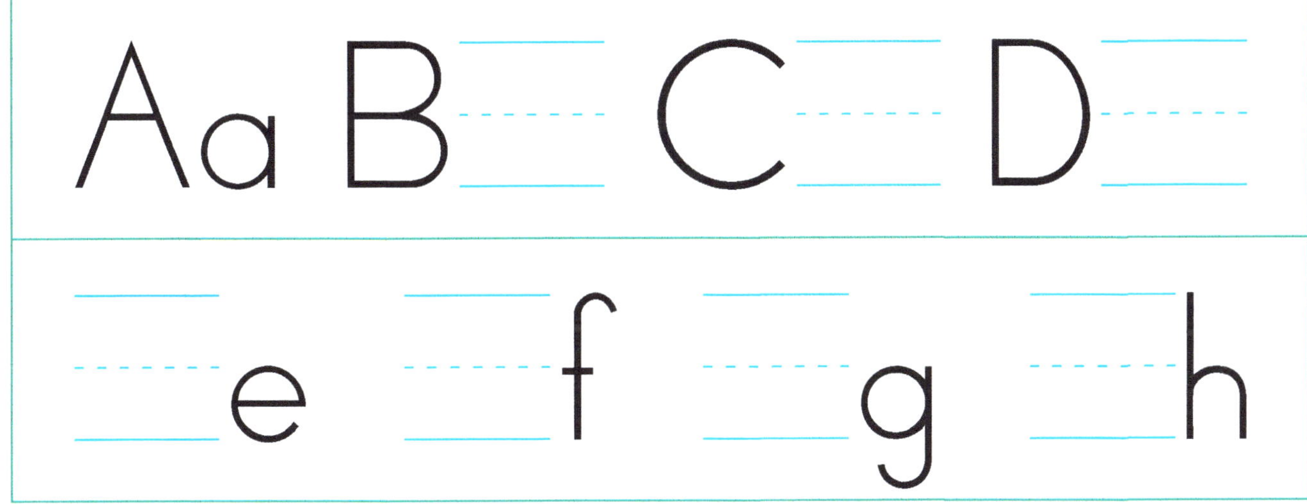

© Continental Press

I	J	K	L
m	n	o	p
Q	R	S	T
u	v	w	x
Y	Z		

Sometimes

Sometimes
when I skip or hop
or when I'm
    jumping
Suddenly
I like to stop
and listen to me
    thumping.

Lilian Moore

Dear Family,

Our class is beginning to learn the sounds that letters stand for. In this book you will see some letters between slashes, like this /s/. That means the sound (ssss) rather than the name of the letter, s. We are starting with the letters **s**, **m**, **b**, **t**, **f**, and **r**, and we'll learn many words that begin with those sounds. Then we will add two vowel sounds, short **a** (cat) and short **i** (sit). With those eight letters your child will be able to read many short words.

This is a very exciting time for a child. Most children are eager to learn to read by themselves. You can help your child in many ways. Here are a couple of ideas.

- Ask your child to name pictures of simple things and tell you the first sound in the word. Then ask for other things that begin with the same sound.
- Make the sound of any of the letters above, and help your child write the letter. Then you can add letters to make a word. (f→ish)
- Read the poem on the other side of this page aloud and help your child find the words that begin with the letter **s.** Say the words together and listen for the sound /s/. Do the same thing to find words that have the letter **m.**
- There are many good books to read aloud to your child now. Visit the library to find a new favorite.

Name

Super **s**andwich begins with the sound /s/.
We print the letter s for the sound /s/.

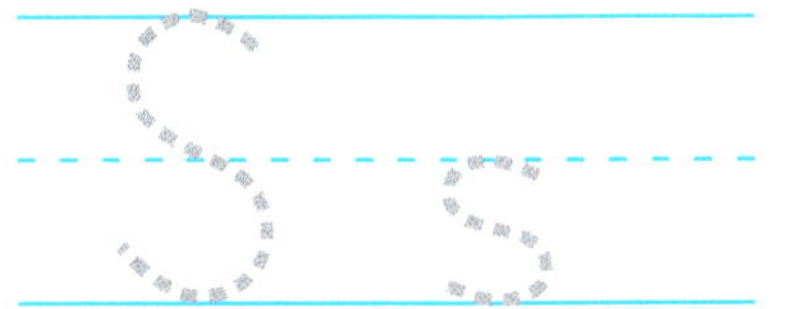

Name each picture.
If it begins with the sound /s/, circle the picture.

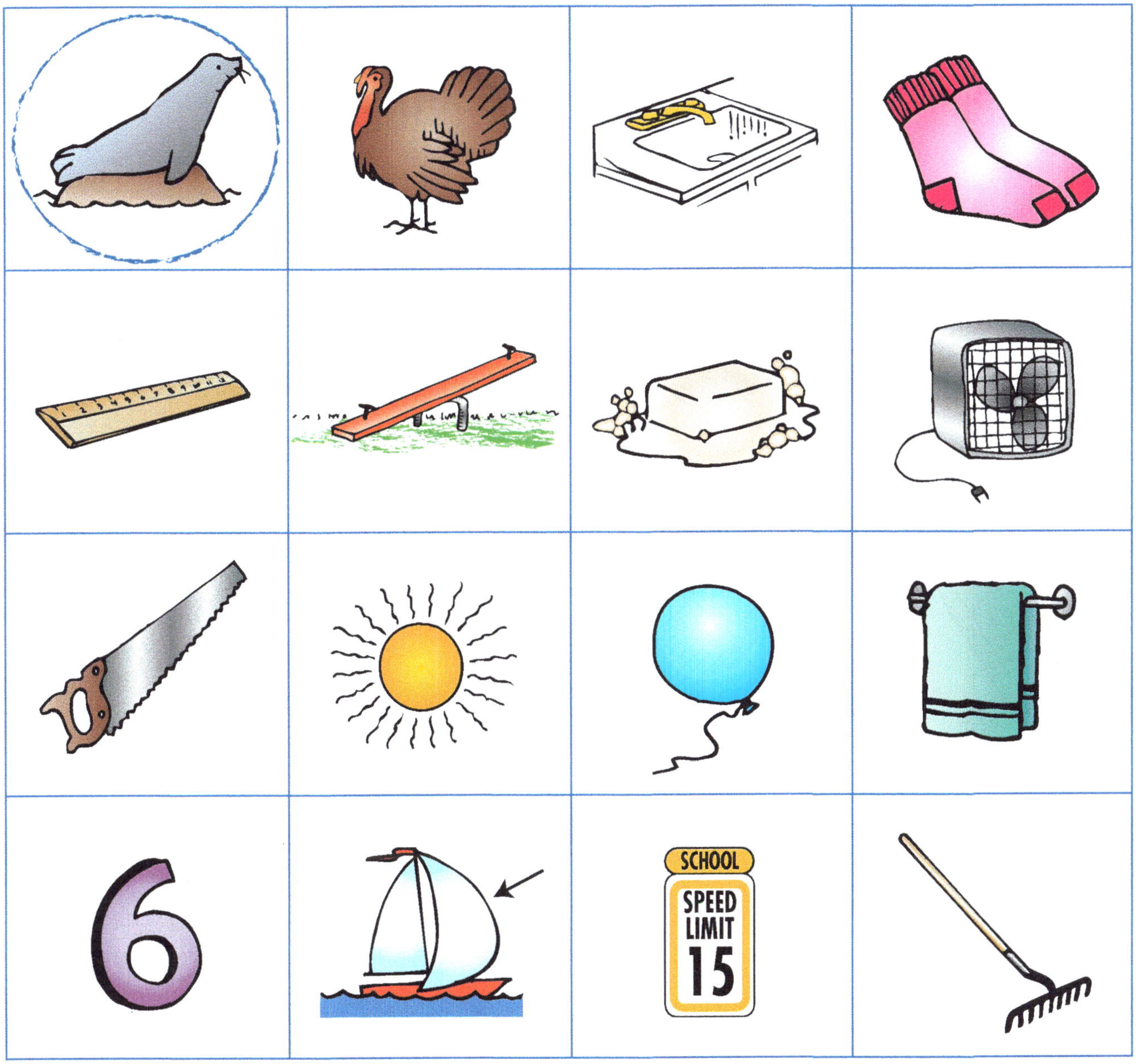

SCHOOL
SPEED LIMIT 15

© Continental Press

Muffin **m**an begins with the sound /m/.
We print the letter m for the sound /m/.

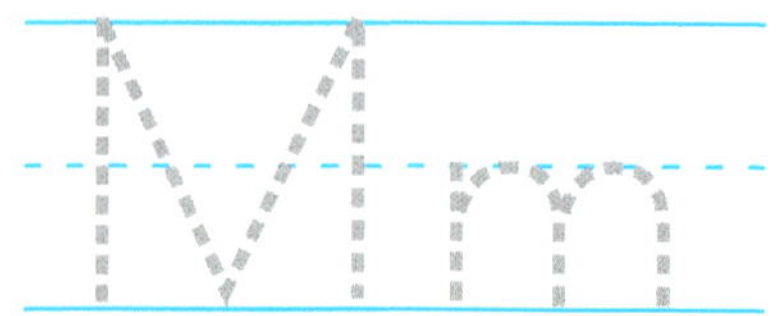

Name each picture.
If it begins with the sound /m/, circle the picture.

Name

Name each picture.
If it begins with /m/ as in **m**uffin **m**an, print m.
If it begins with /s/ as in **s**uper **s**andwich, print s.

© Continental Press

Name each picture.
If it begins with /m/ as in **m**uffin **m**an, print m.
If it begins with /s/ as in **s**uper **s**andwich, print s.

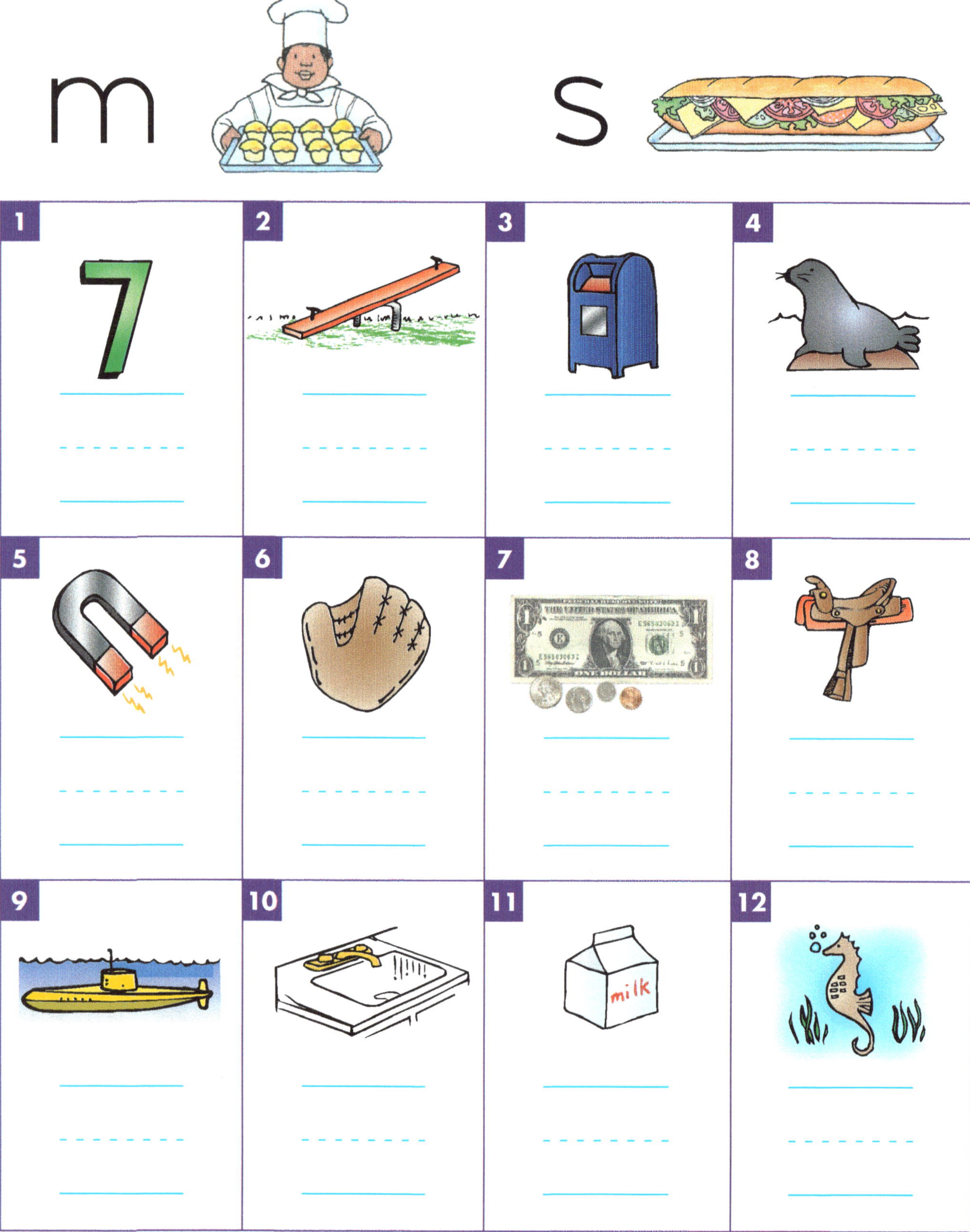

Name

Tiny **t**axi begins with the sound /t/.
We print the letter t for the sound /t/.

Name each picture.
If it begins with the sound /t/, circle the picture.

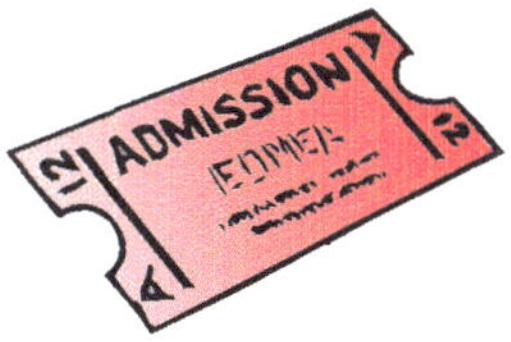

© Continental Press

Bumblebee begins with the sound /b/.
We print the letter b for the sound /b/.

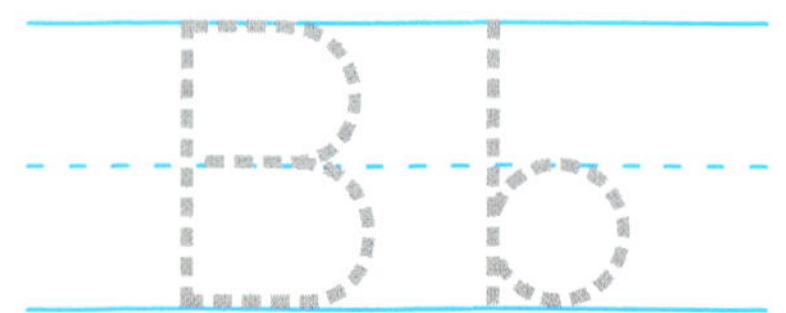

Name each picture.
If it begins with the sound /b/, circle the picture.

Name

Name each picture.
If it begins with /b/ as in **b**umblebee, print b.
If it begins with /t/ as in **t**iny **t**axi, print t.

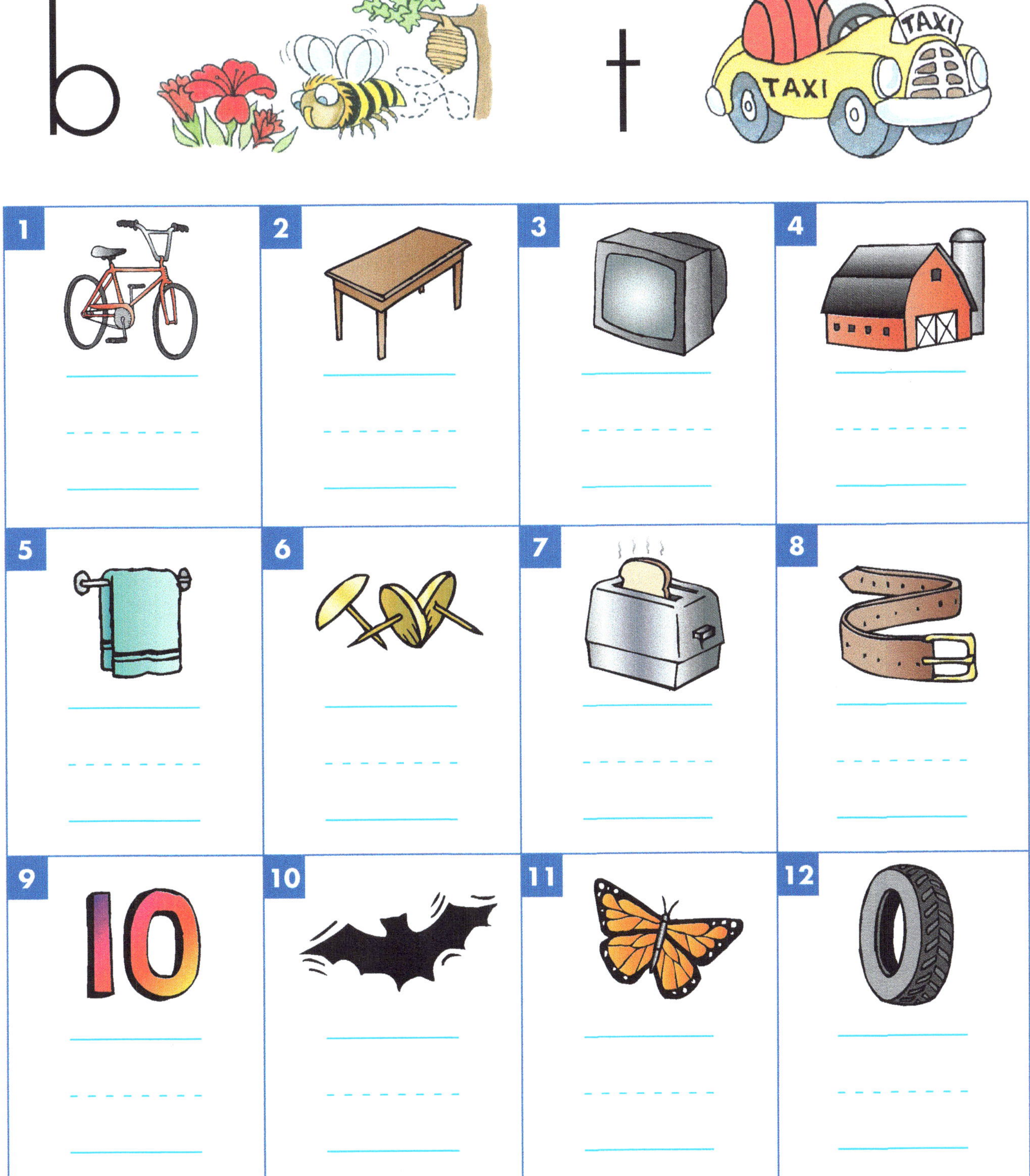

© Continental Press

Name each picture.
If it begins with /b/ as in **b**umblebee, print b.
If it begins with /t/ as in **t**iny **t**axi, print t.

Name

Name each picture.
Print the letter for its beginning sound.

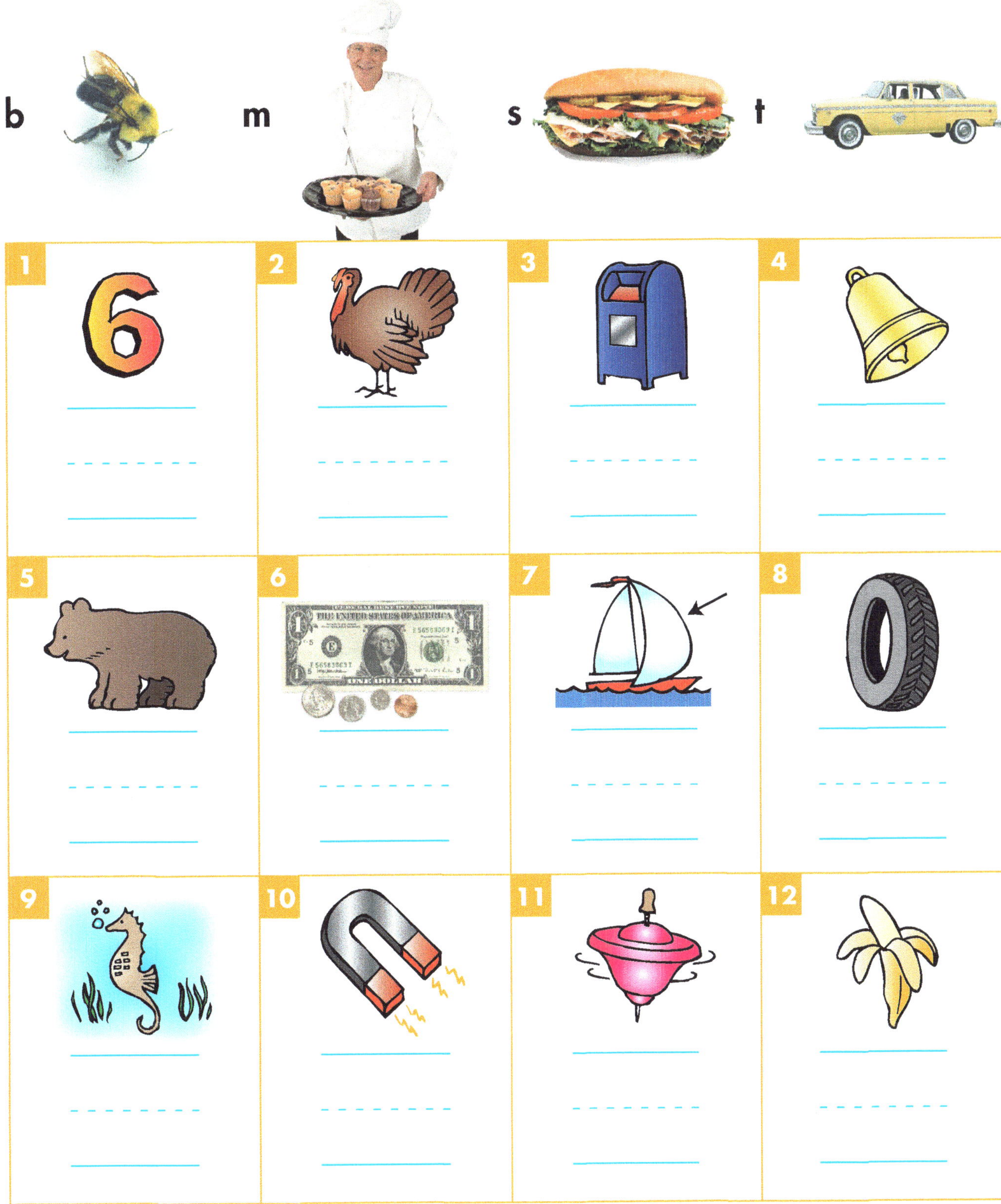

© Continental Press

Name each picture.
Circle the letter for its beginning sound.
Print the letter to complete the word.

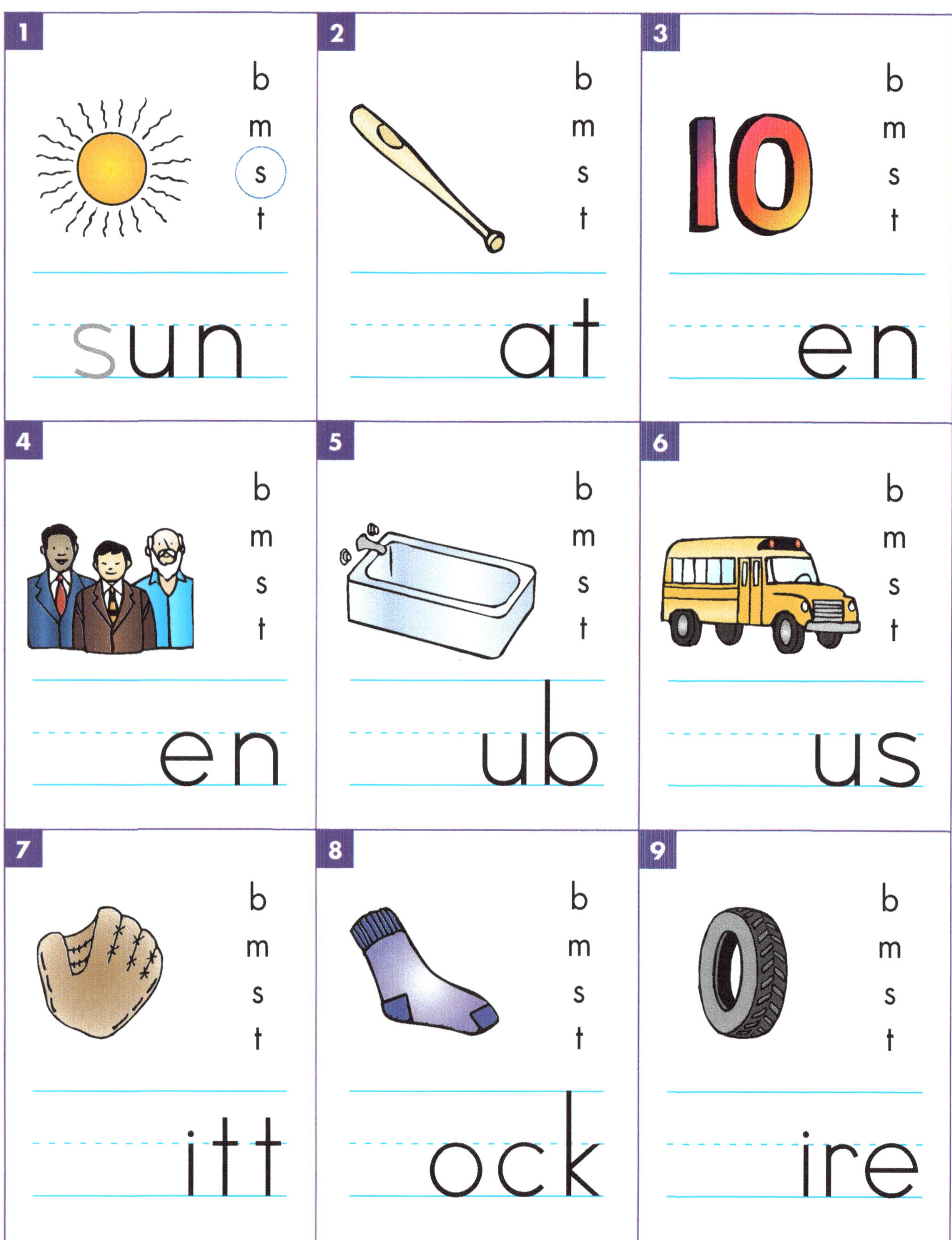

Associating initial sounds with letters in words: **b, m, s, t**

Name

Fancy **f**ish begins with the sound /f/.
We print the letter f for the sound /f/.

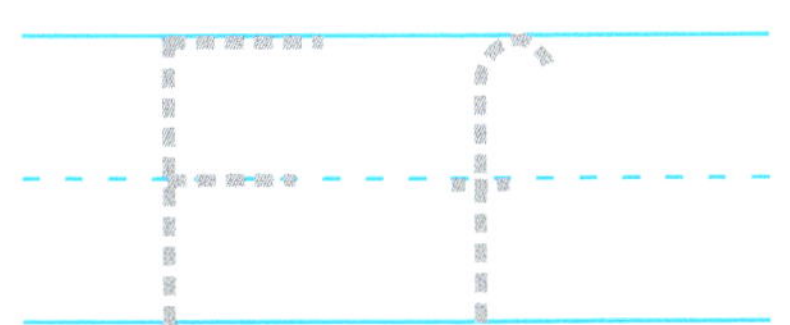

Name each picture.
If it begins with the sound /f/, circle the picture.

© Continental Press

Remarkable **r**obot begins with the sound /r/.
We print the letter r for the sound /r/.

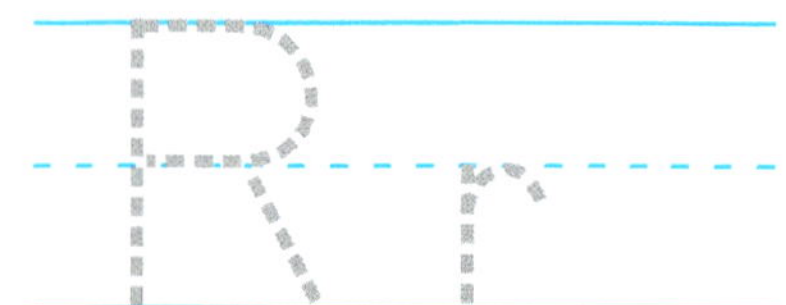

Name each picture.
If it begins with the sound /r/, circle the picture.

Name

Name each picture.
If it begins with /f/ as in **f**ancy **f**ish, print f.
If it begins with /r/ as in **r**emarkable **r**obot, print r.

© Continental Press

Name each picture.
Print the letter for its beginning sound.

Associating initial sounds with letters: **b, f, r, t**

Name

Name the pictures in each row.
If the picture name begins with the sound of the letter,
fill in the circle under the picture.

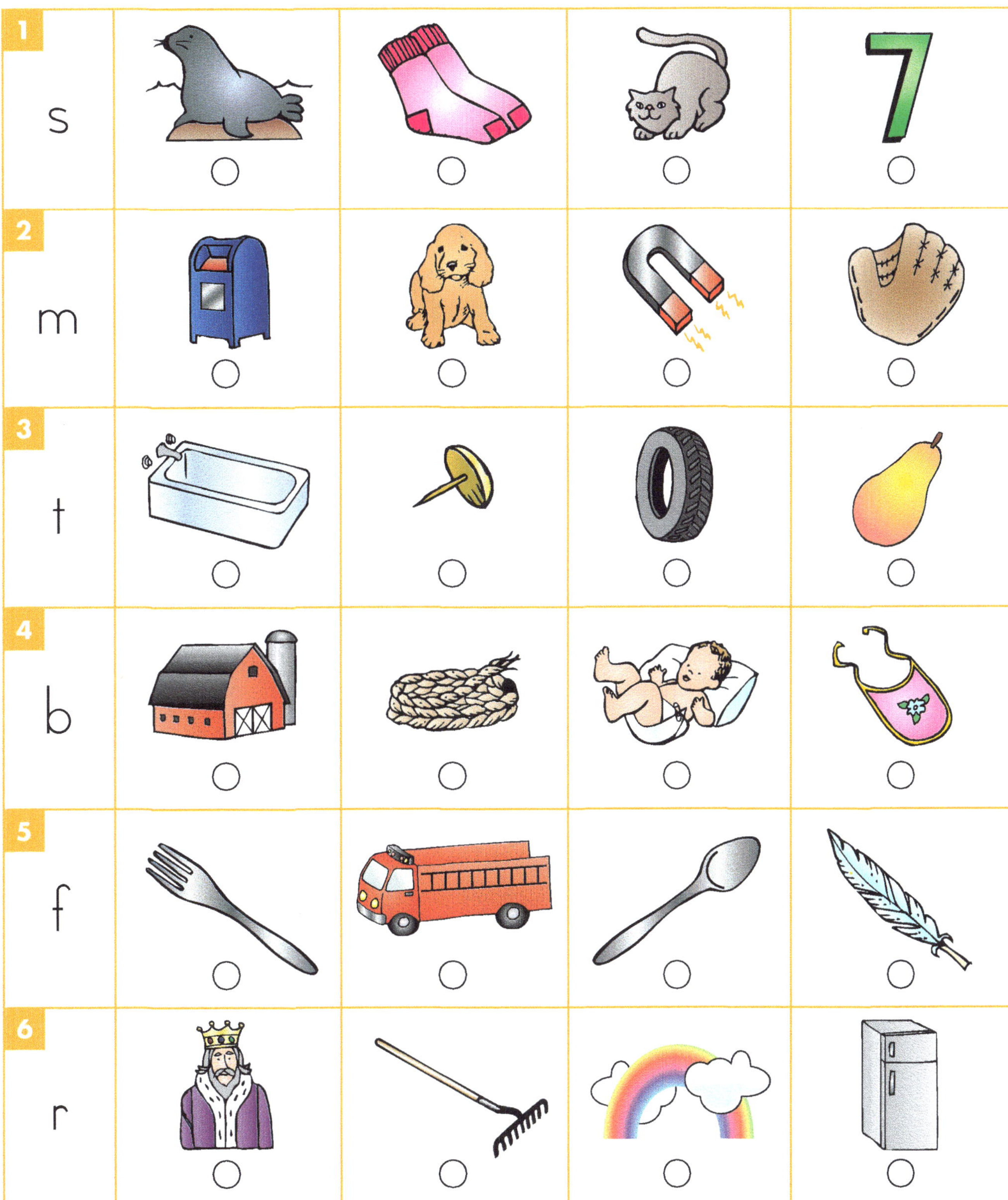

© Continental Press

Review initial consonants: **b, f, m, r, s, t**

Name each picture.
Circle the letter for its beginning sound.
Print the letter to complete the word.

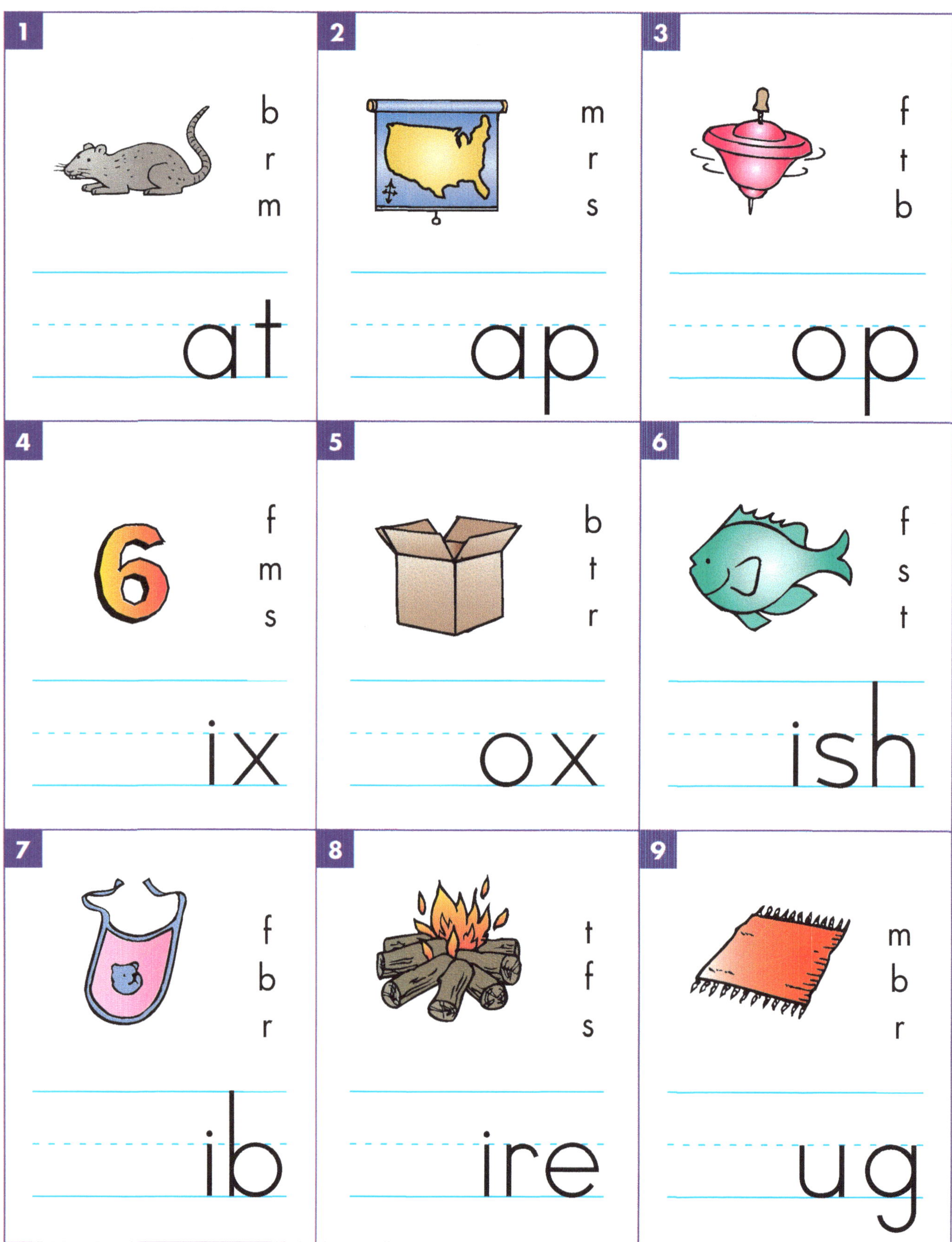

Associating initial sounds with letters in words: **b, f, m, r, s, t**

Name

Abby begins with the short **a** sound.
C**a**t has the short **a** sound in the middle.

A a

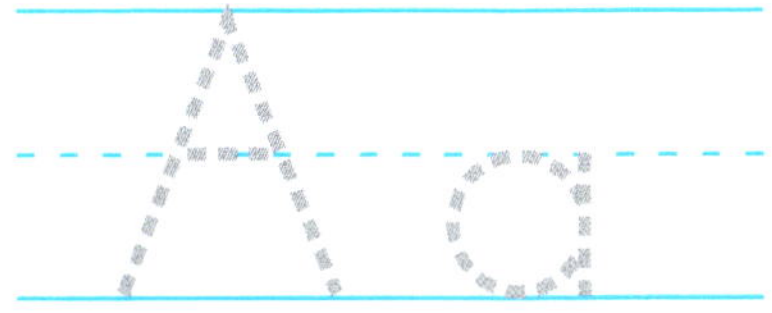

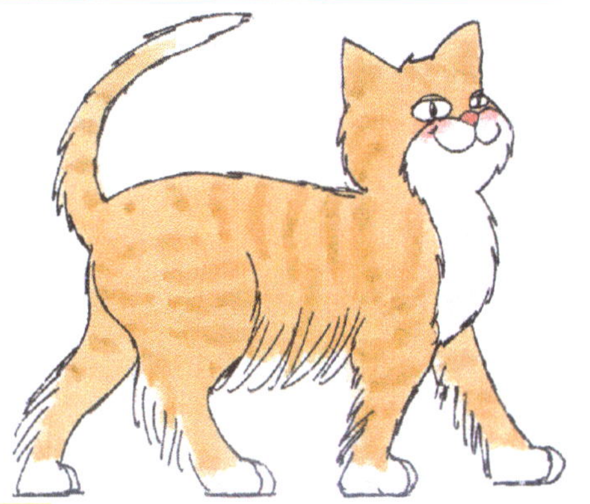

Name each picture. Circle the picture if you hear the short **a** sound at the beginning or in the middle.

This is **A**bby the c**a**t.

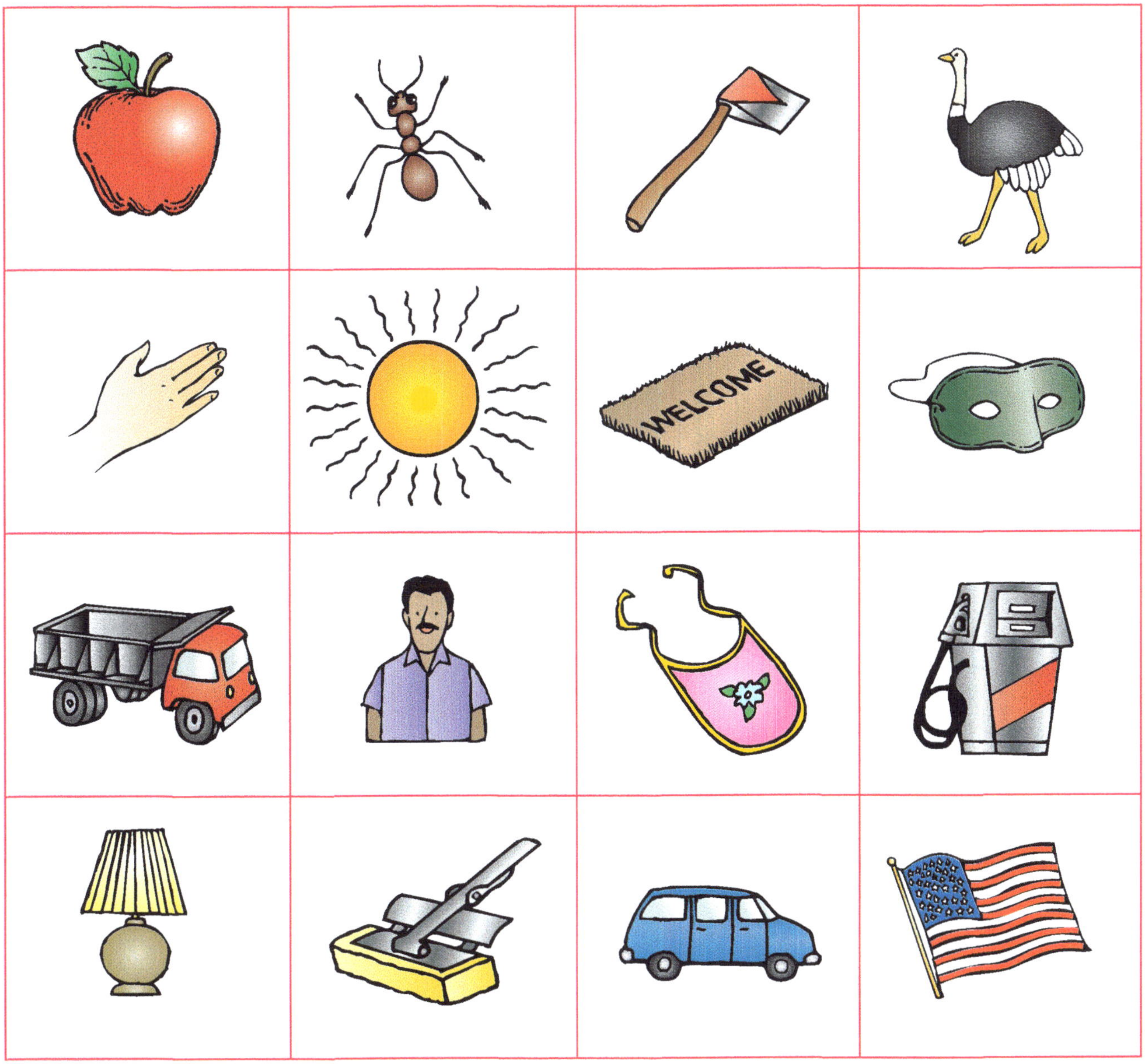

© Continental Press

Name each picture.
Print a if you hear the short **a** sound in the middle.

1	2	3
b a g	c p	p n

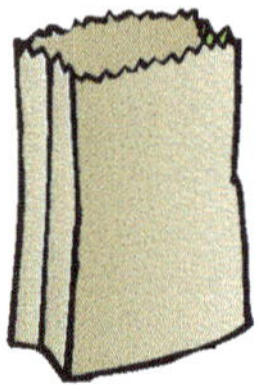

4	5	6
m p	b x	f n

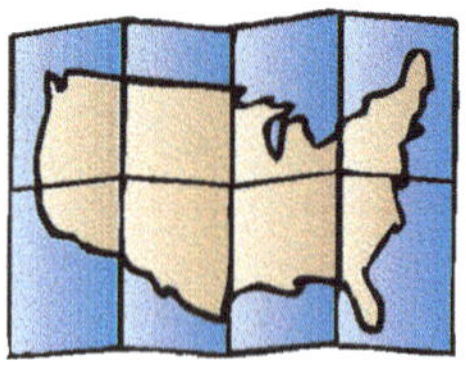

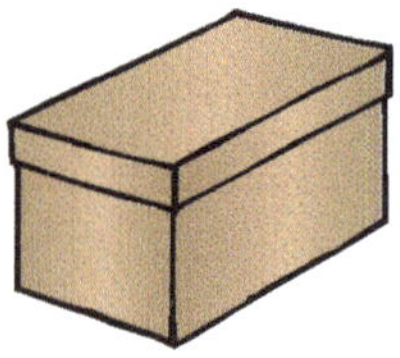

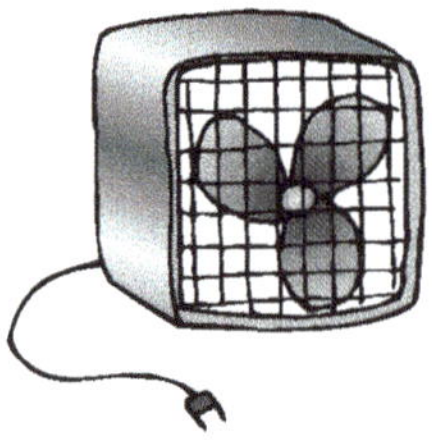

7	8	9
p g	c n	t g

Associating vowel sounds with letters: short **a**

Name

Say the sound for the first letter.
Blend it with –**at**.
Print the word you say on the line.
Draw a line to the picture for the word.

m at

r at

b at

f at

© *Continental Press*

cat ram

Name each picture.
Print at or am to complete each picture name.

h

b

j

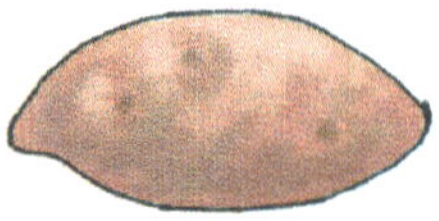

y

f

r

Name

Ickle begins with the short **i** sound.
Pi**g** has the short **i** sound in the middle.

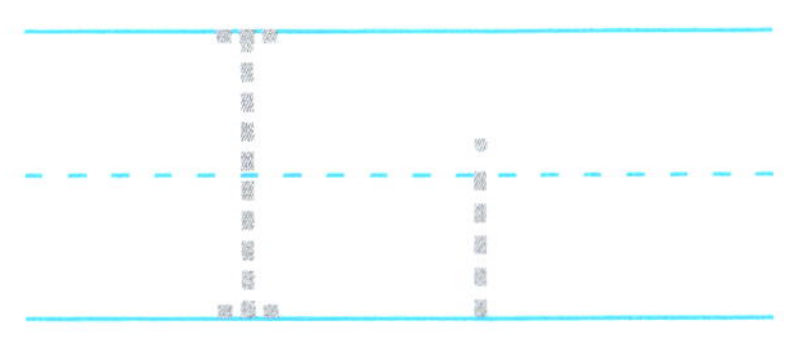

This is **I**ckle the pi**g**.

Name each picture. Circle the picture if you hear the short **i** sound at the beginning or in the middle.

© Continental Press

Name each picture.
Print i if you hear the short **i** sound in the middle.

1	2	3
b ___ b	w ___ g	k ___ t

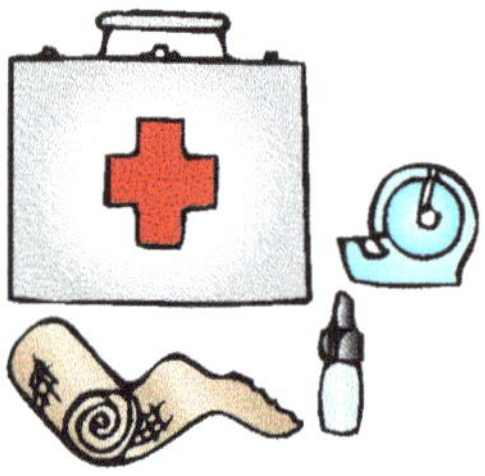

4	5	6
b ___ g	p ___ n	s ___ x

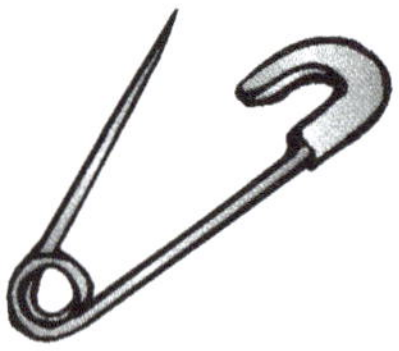

7	8	9
p ___ g	m ___ p	l ___ d

Name

Say the sound for the first letter.
Blend it with **–it**.
Print the word you say on the line.
Draw a line to the picture for the word.

s it

b it

f it

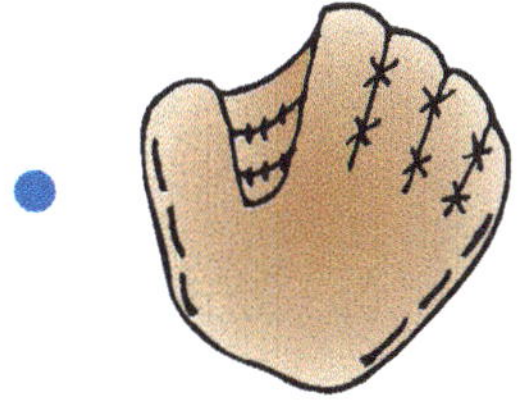

m itt

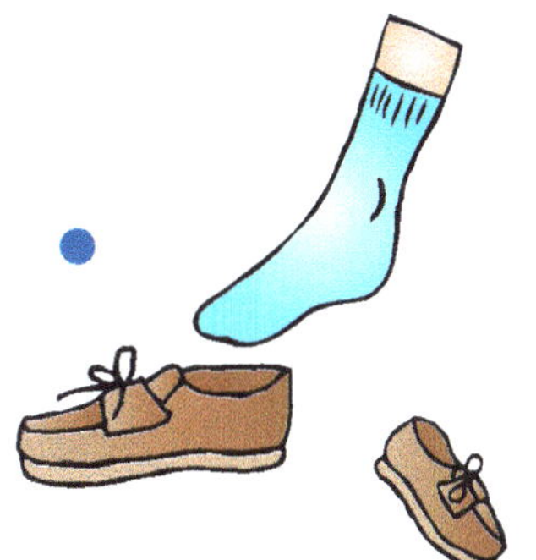

© Continental Press

bit

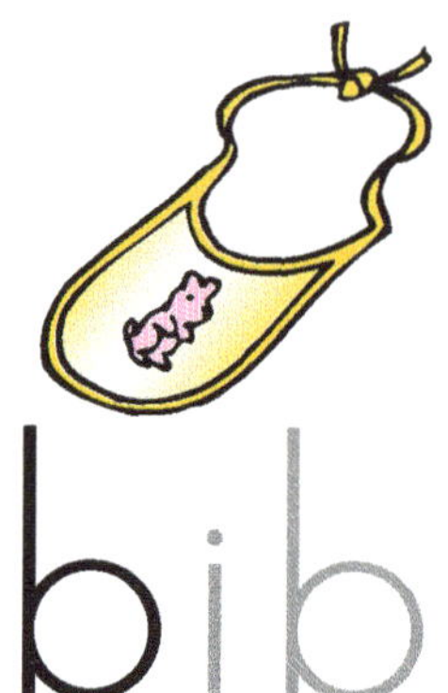

bib

Name each picture.
Complete the picture name by printing it or ib.

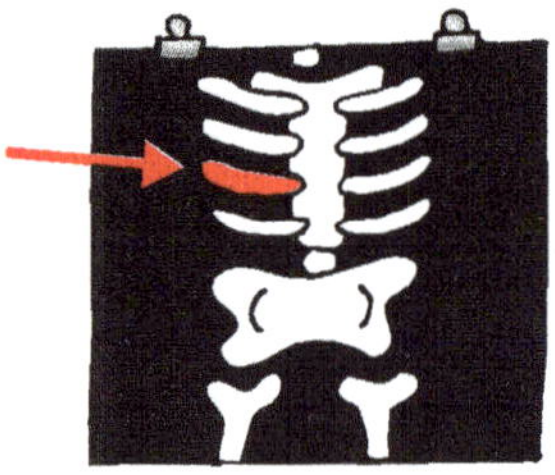

r

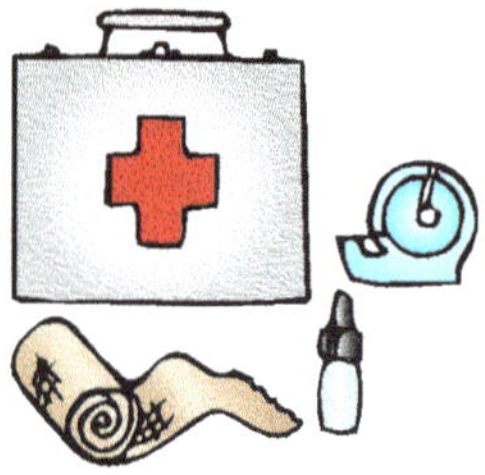

k

s

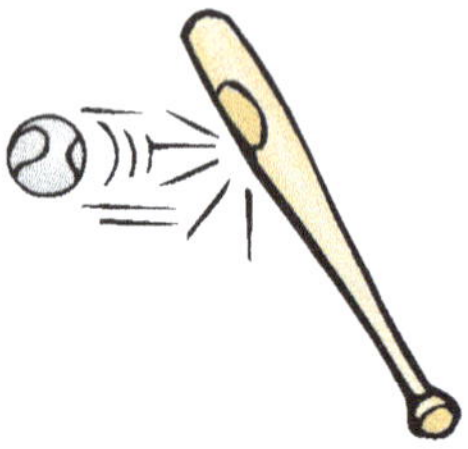

h

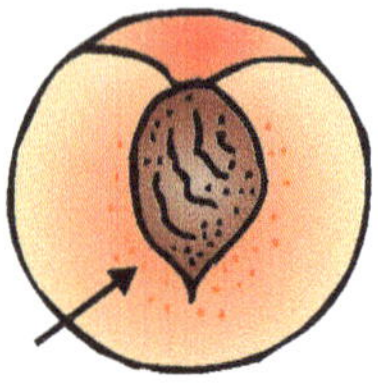

p

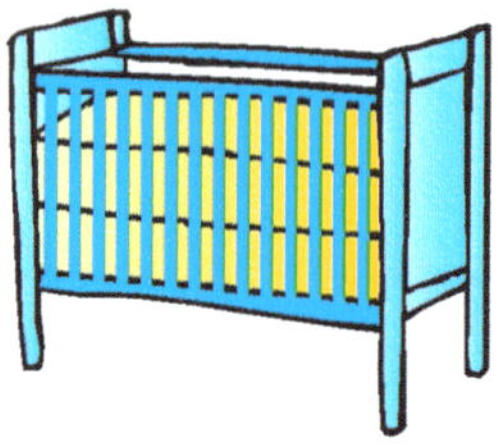

cr

Name

Name each picture. Look at the words beside the picture.
Circle the word with the same middle sound.
Print the letter to complete the word.

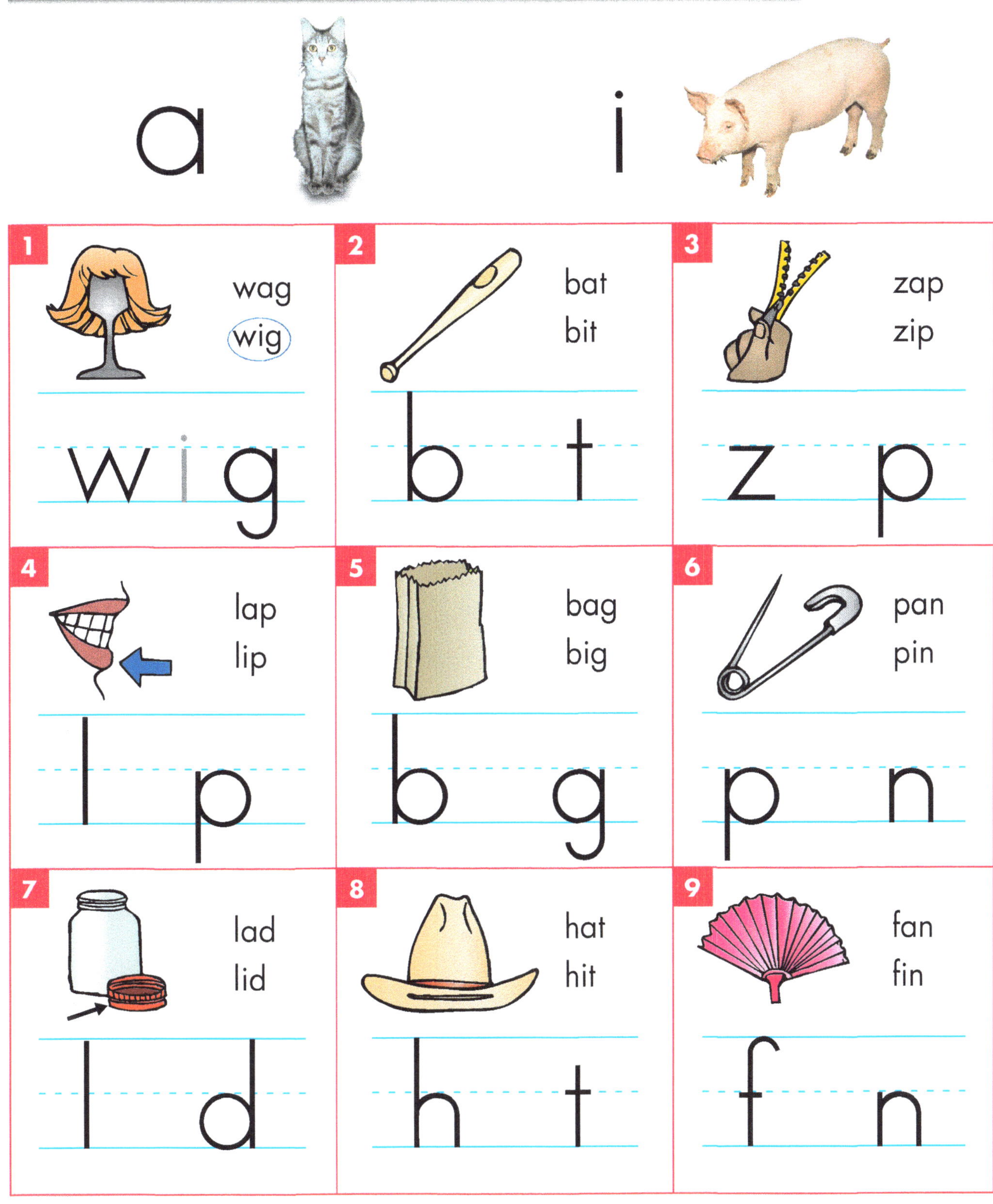

© Continental Press

Name each picture.
Circle the letter for the sound at the end of the word.
Print the letter to complete the word.

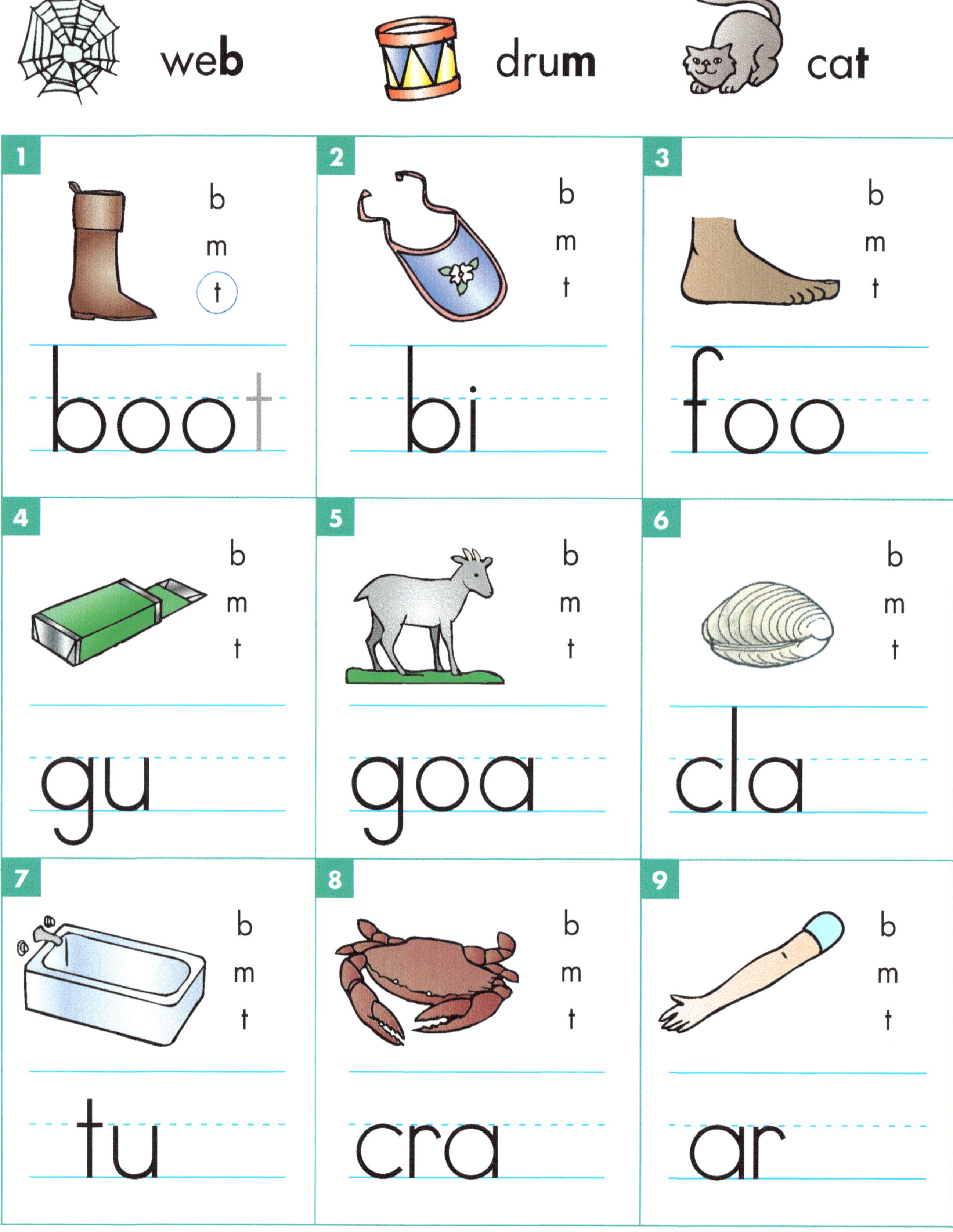

Associating final sounds with letters in words: **b, m, t**

Name

Read each word. Draw a line to its picture.
Print the word beside the picture.

ram

sit

bib

rat

bat

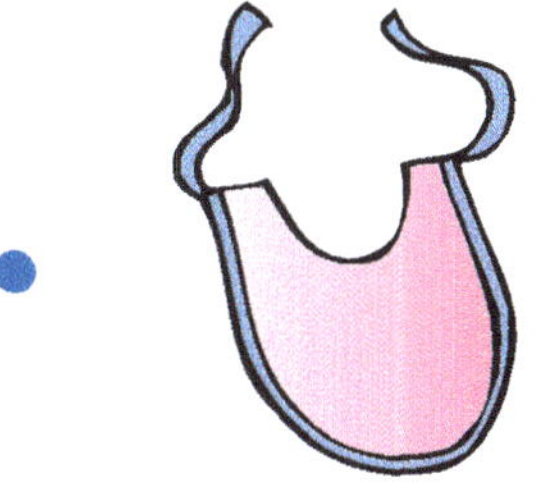

© Continental Press

Read the phrases.
Circle the phrase that goes with each picture.
Print the phrase under each picture.

a cat in a hat

a fat ram

a rat at bat

a pin on a hat

a big bag

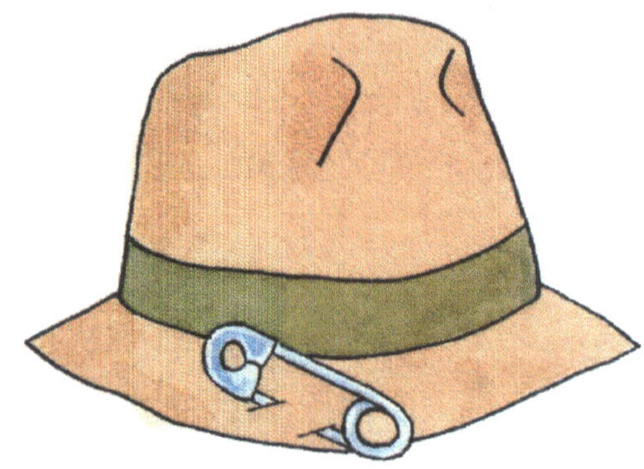

8 Go fast, Bib!

At Bat

1

fold

cut

6 Go, Sam!

Tim has a mitt. 3

© Continental Press

2 Sam has a fat bat.

Go, Tim! **7**

4 Bib sits on a mat.

Sam is at bat. **5**

Unit 2 Progress Check

Name ______________________

Listen to the name of each picture.
Circle the letter for its beginning sound.

© Continental Press

Unit 2 Progress Check

Listen to each word.
Find the word in the box and circle it.

1	2	3	4	5
tab	rim	Fat	bib	Sam
bit	ram	Sam	rib	Tam
bat	rat	Sat	bit	Tim

6	7	8	9	10
bit	mat	fib	mat	bib
sat	ram	bib	rat	bat
sit	tam	fit	fat	bit

11	12	13	14	15
fab	rib	Sit	fat	rat
fat	rat	Sam	fit	rim
rat	rim	Sat	sit	tam

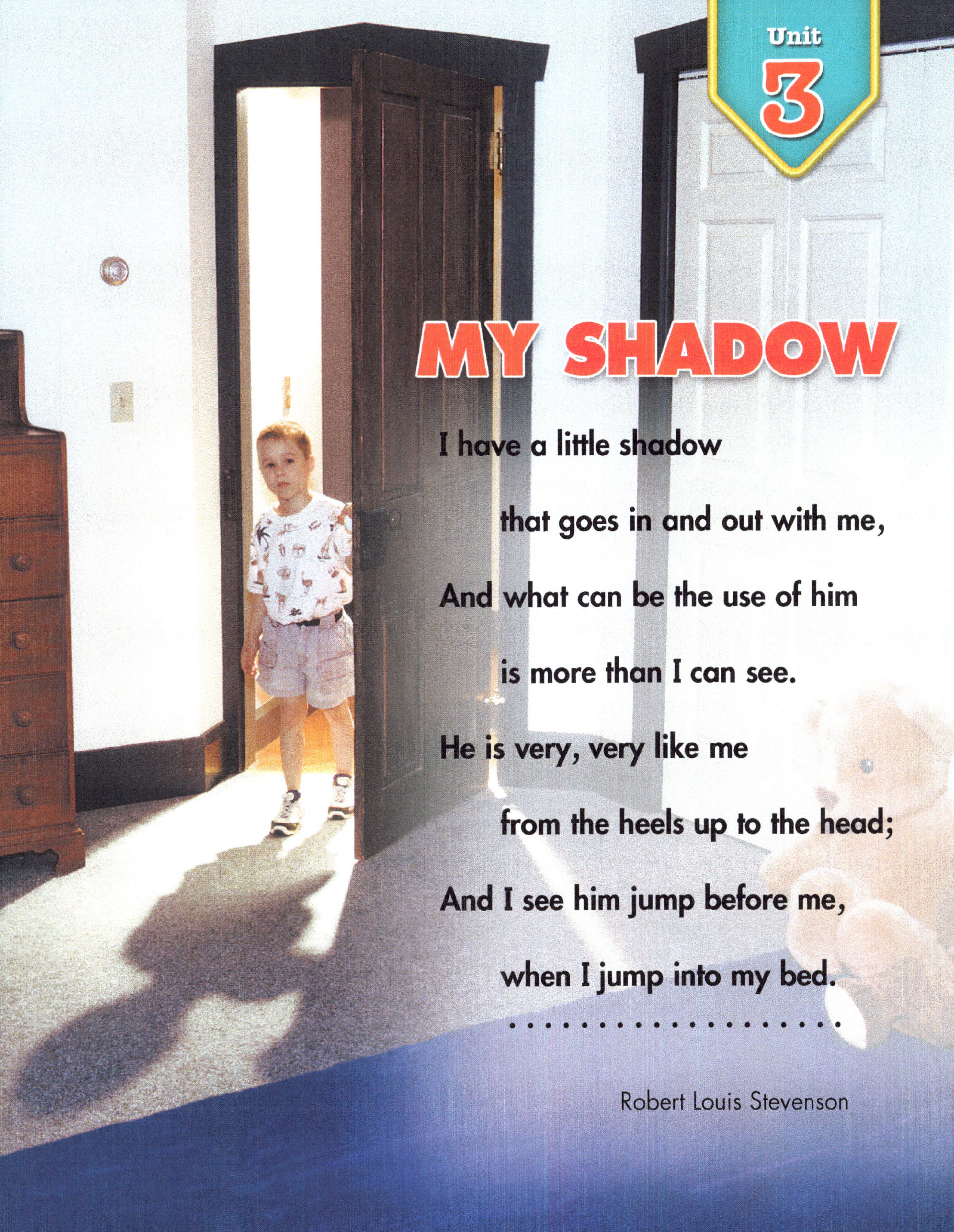

Unit 3

MY SHADOW

I have a little shadow
that goes in and out with me,
And what can be the use of him
is more than I can see.
He is very, very like me
from the heels up to the head;
And I see him jump before me,
when I jump into my bed.
. . . .

Robert Louis Stevenson

Dear Family,

Our class is learning more about the sounds of letters. We are now learning the sounds the letters **n**, **p**, **d**, **h**, **c**, and **g** stand for and many words that begin with those sounds. Then we will add two more vowel sounds; short **o** (hop) and short **e** (hen). With all of these sounds and letters, your child will be able to read many words and even some short stories.

Here are a few ways that you can help your child at home.

- When your child brings home a booklet such as the story "At Bat," take time to listen and read along. Most children are eager to learn to read, and will appreciate your praise and interest in their new reading skills.
- Make the sound any of the letters above stand for, and have your child write the letter. Then you can add letters to make a word. (n→est)
- Read the poem on the other side of this page aloud. Help your child find words that begin with the letters **a**, **b**, **c**, **g**, **h**, or **m**. See how many of these words your child can read. Give help as needed.
- Some books you will enjoy reading together include *Daniel's Duck* by Clyde Bulla, *The Very Hungry Caterpillar* by Eric Carle, and *Goggles!* by Ezra Jack Keats.

Name

Number **n**ine begins with the sound /n/.
We print the letter n for the sound /n/.

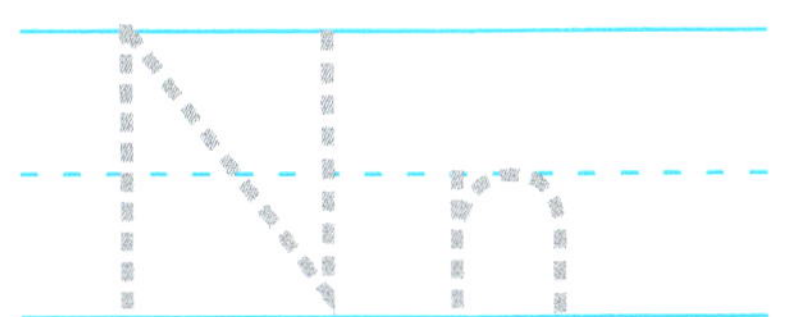

Name each picture.
If it begins with the sound /n/, circle the picture.

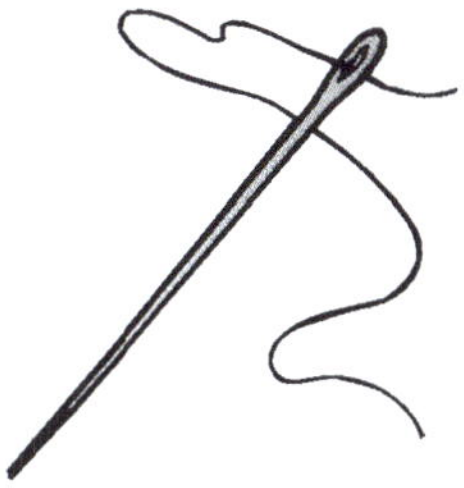

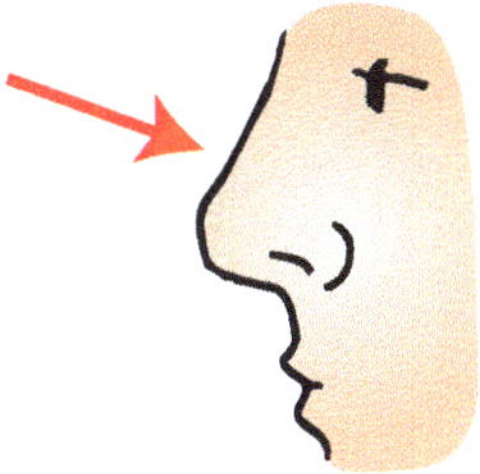

© Continental Press

Polly **p**arrot begins with the sound /p/.
We print the letter p for the sound /p/.

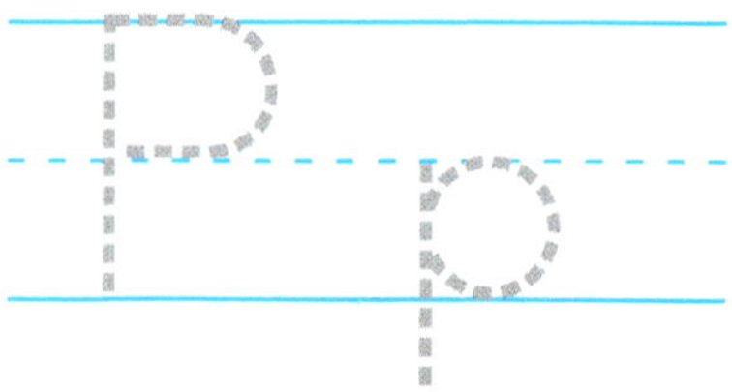

P p

Name each picture.
If it begins with the sound /p/, circle the picture.

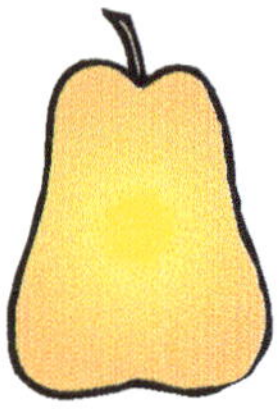

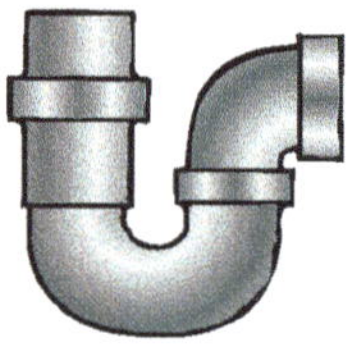

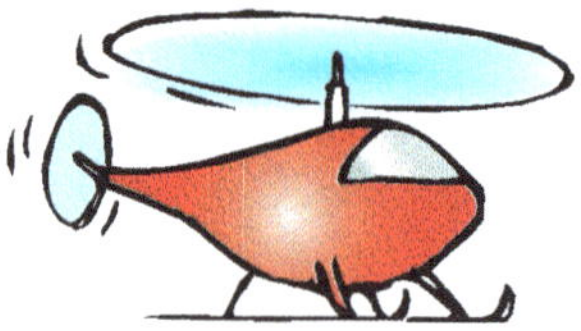

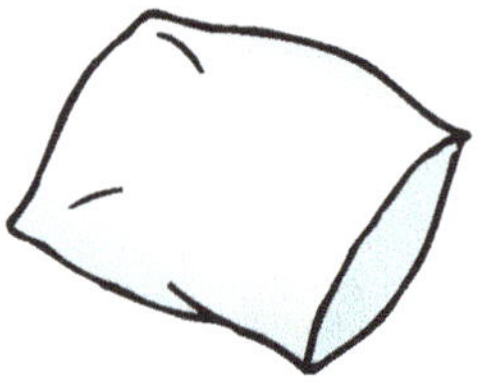

Name

Name each picture.
If it begins with /n/ as in **n**umber **n**ine, print n.
If it begins with /p/ as in **P**olly **p**arrot, print p.

© Continental Press

Name each picture.
Circle the word that begins with the same sound.
Print the first letter to finish the picture name.

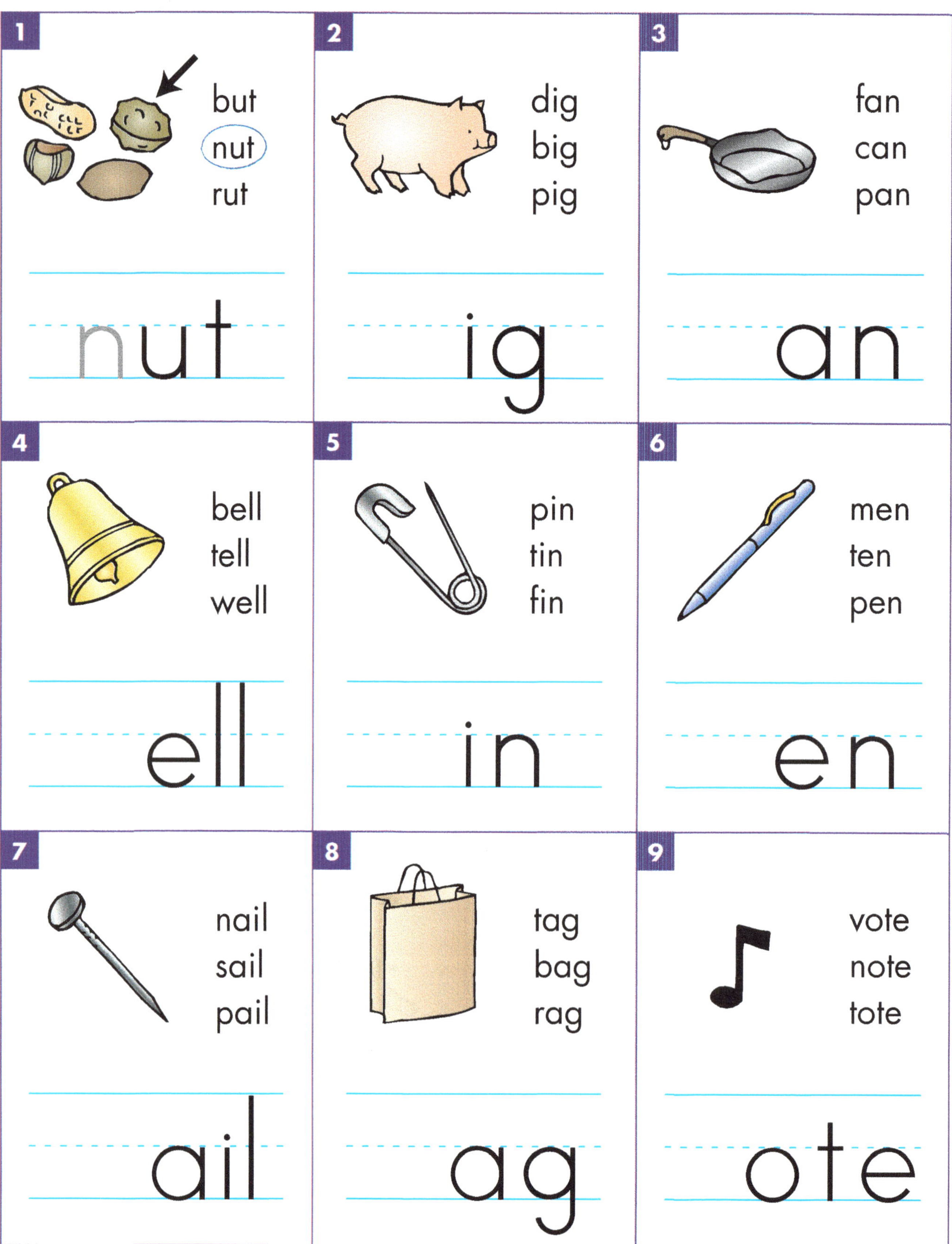

Associating initial sounds with letters in words: **b, n, p**

Name

Diving **d**uck begins with the sound /d/.
We print the letter d for the sound /d/.

D d

Name each picture.
If it begins with the sound /d/, circle the picture.

© Continental Press

Hungry **h**ippo begins with the sound /h/.
We print the letter h for the sound /h/.

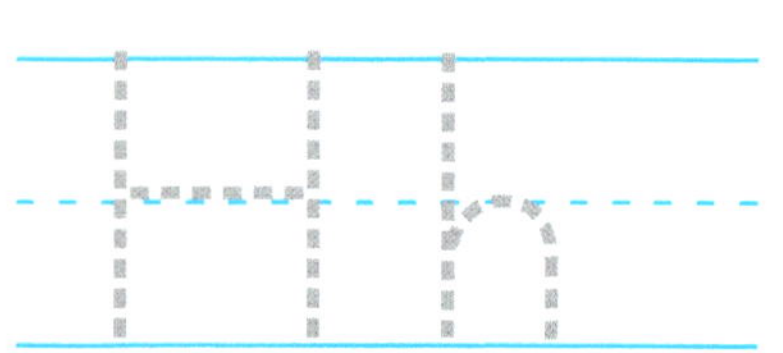

Name each picture.
If it begins with the sound /h/, circle the picture.

Name

Name each picture.
If it begins with /d/ as in **d**iving **d**uck, print d.
If it begins with /h/ as in **h**ungry **h**ippo, print h.

d 

h 

1

2

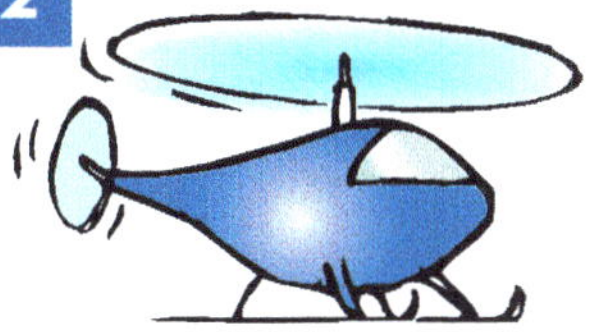

3

4

5

6

7

8

9

10

11

12

© Continental Press

Name each picture.
Print the letter for its beginning sound.

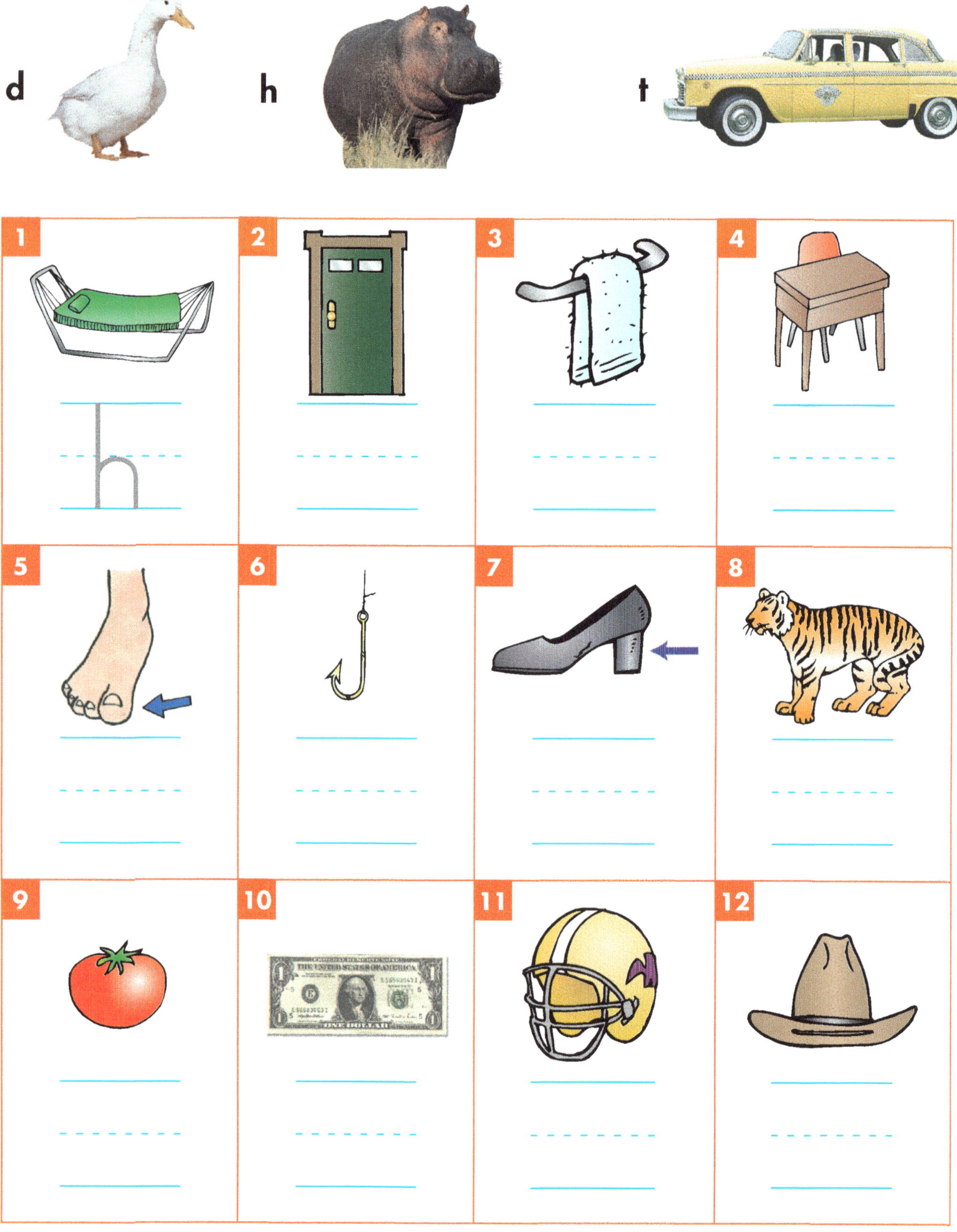

Associating initial sounds with letters: **d** **/d/**, **h** **/h/**, **t** **/t/**

Name

Name the letter and the pictures in each row.
If the picture name begins with the sound of the letter, fill in the circle under the picture.

© Continental Press

Review initial consonants: **d, f, h, n, p, r**

Name each picture.
Circle the word that begins with the same sound.
Print the first letter to finish the picture name.

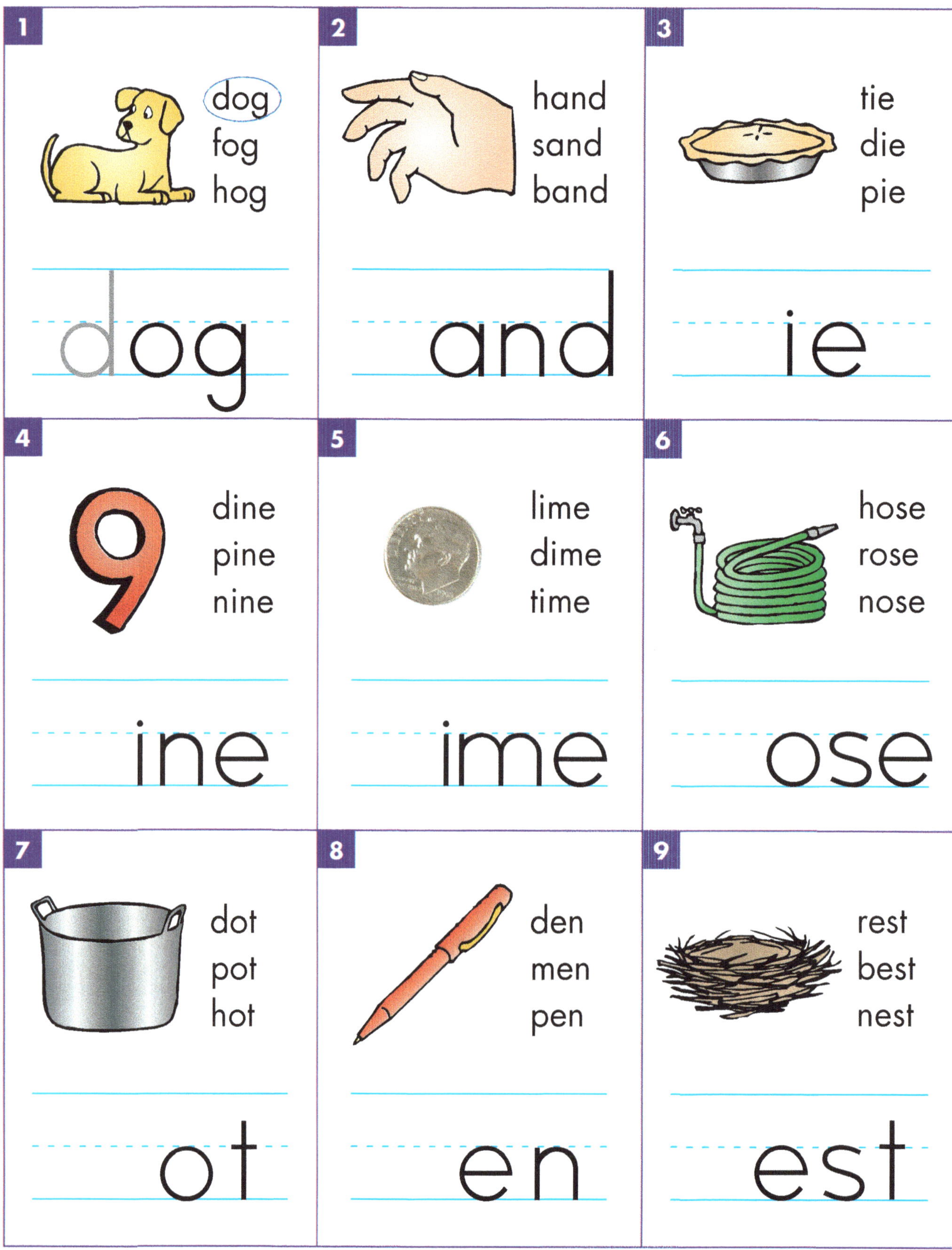

Associating initial sounds with letters in words: **d, h, n, p**

Name

Carrot **c**ake begins with the sound /k/.
We print the letter c for the sound /k/.

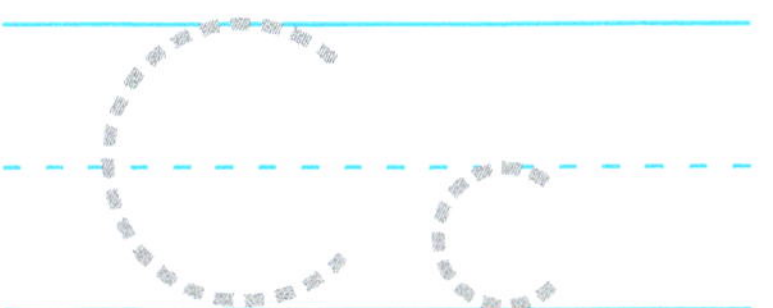

Name each picture.
If it begins with the sound /k/, circle the picture.

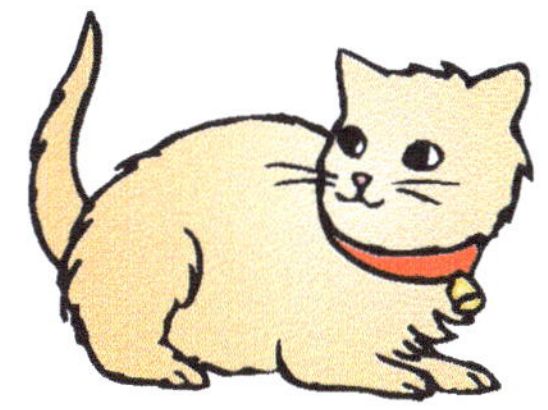

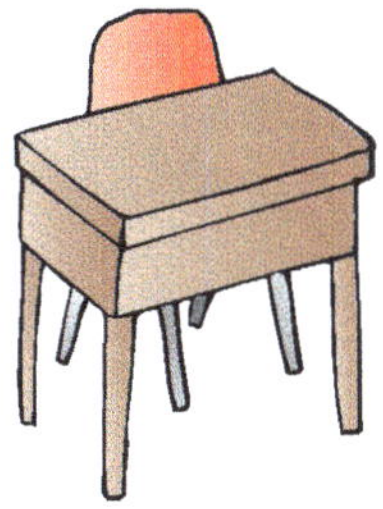

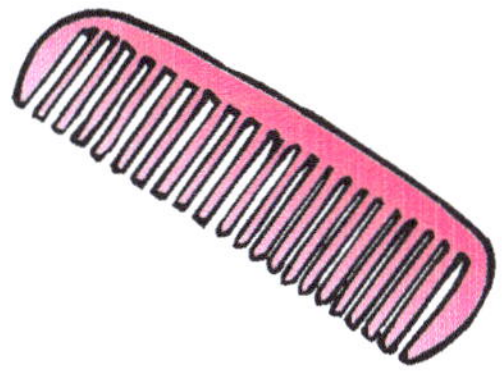

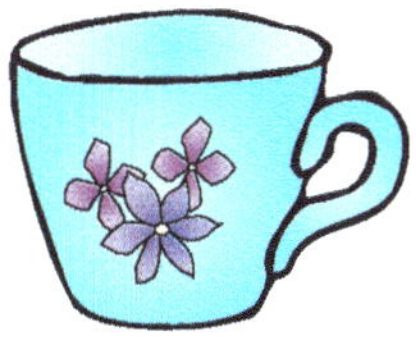

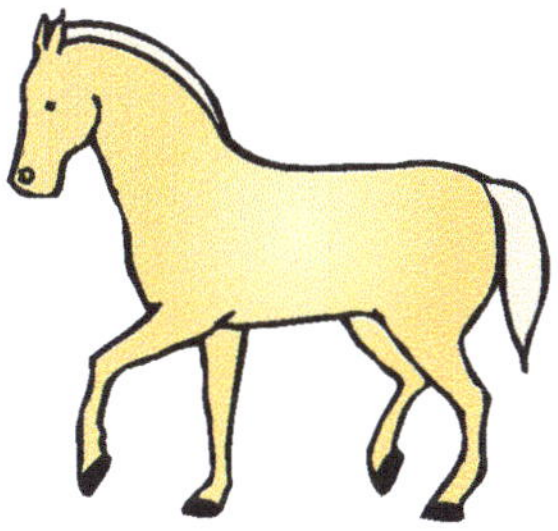

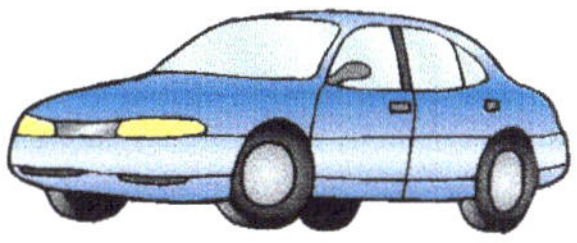

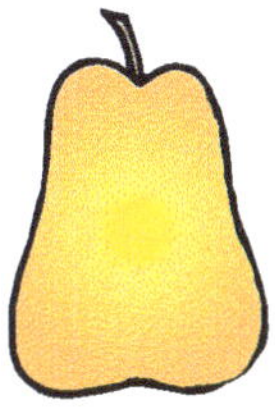

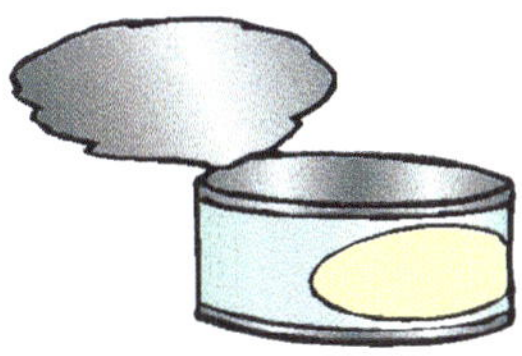

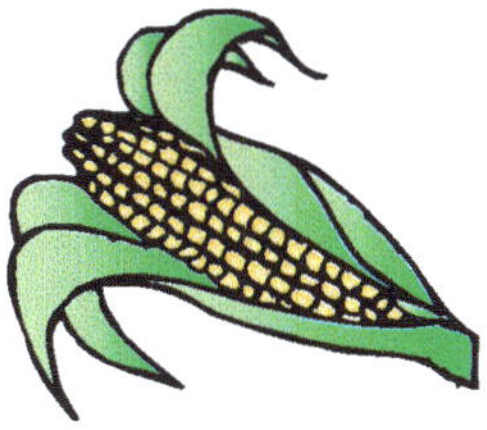

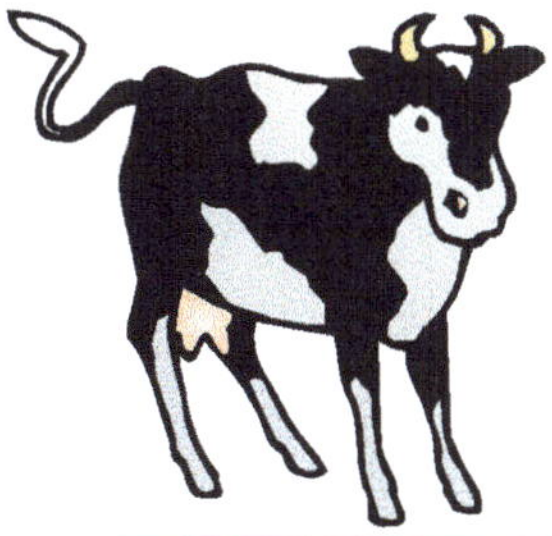

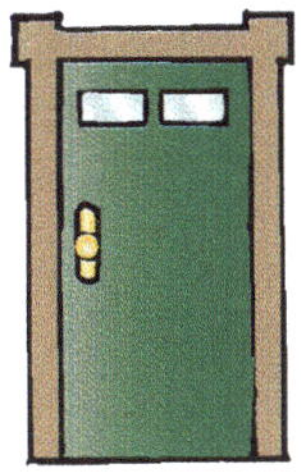

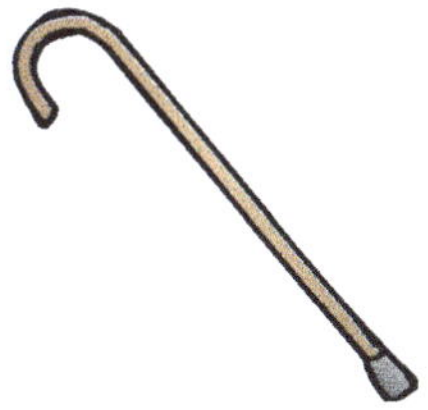

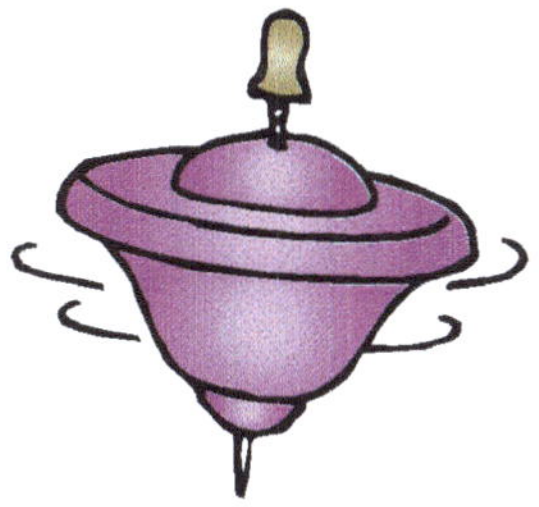

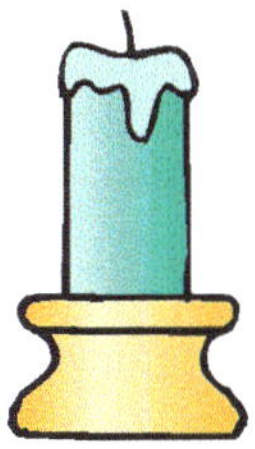

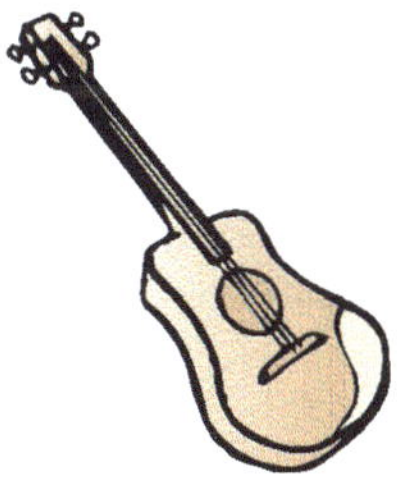

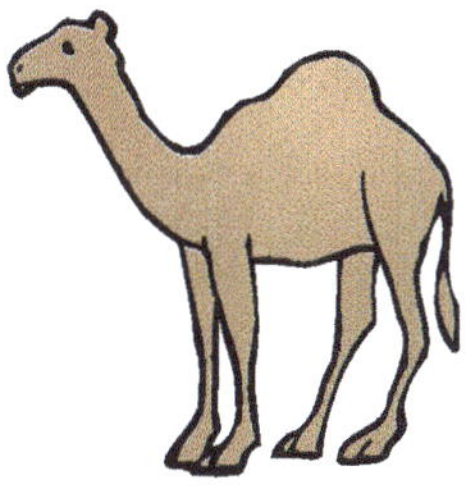

© Continental Press

Galloping **g**oat begins with the sound /g/.
We print the letter g for the sound /g/.

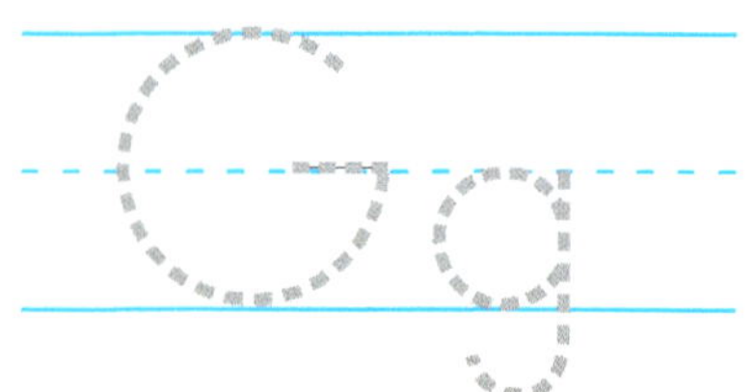

Name each picture.
If it begins with the sound /g/, circle the picture.

Name

Name each picture.
If it begins with /k/ as in **c**arrot **c**ake, print c.
If it begins with /g/ as in **g**alloping **g**oat, print g.

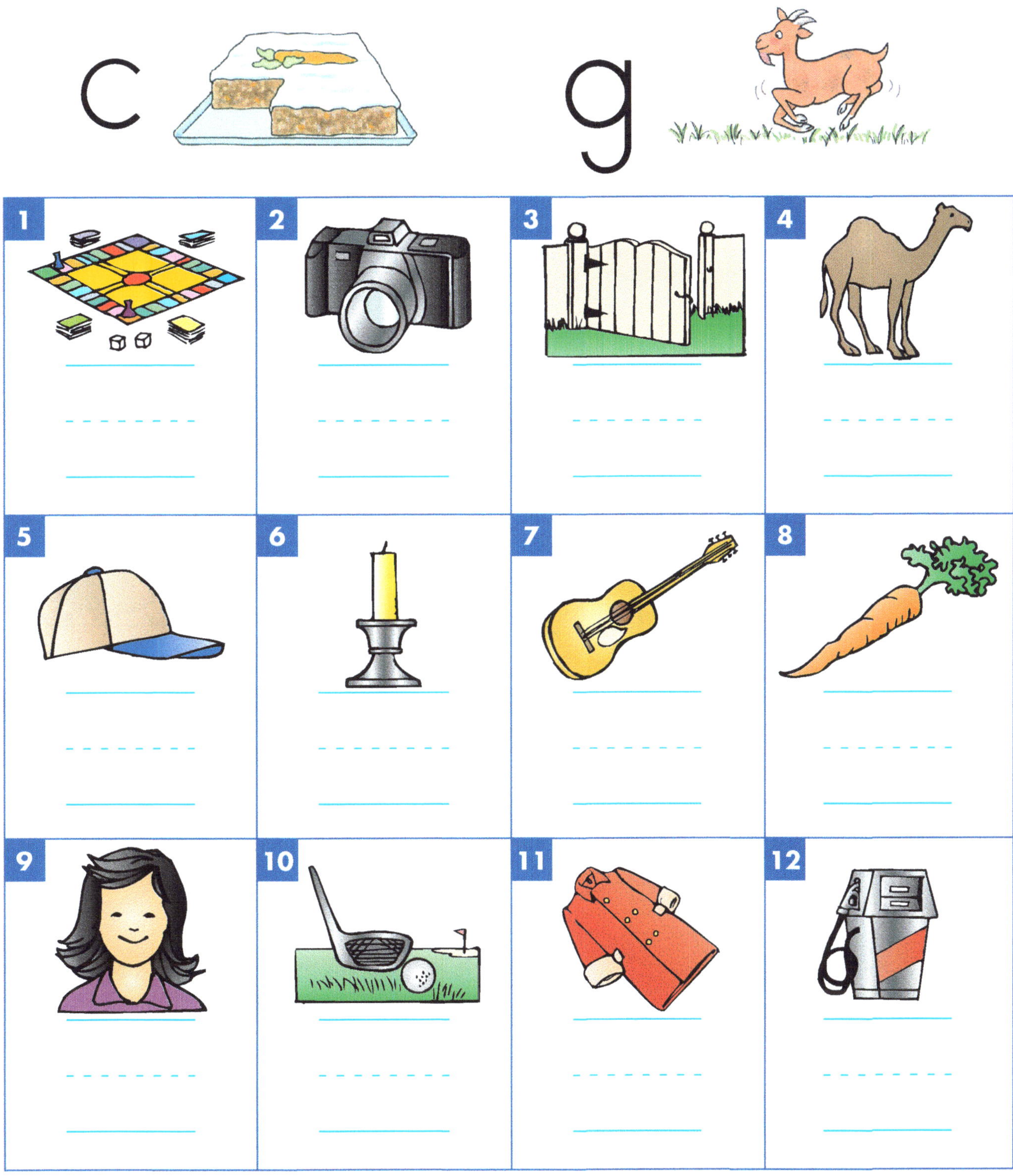

© Continental Press

c d g h n p

Name each picture.
Print the letter for its beginning sound.

1

2

3

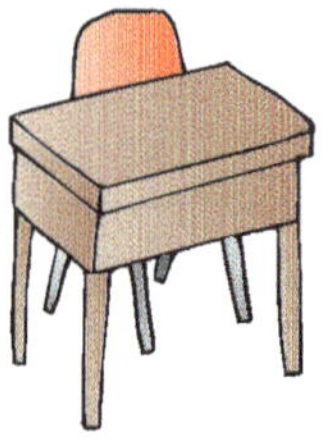

4

5

6

7

8

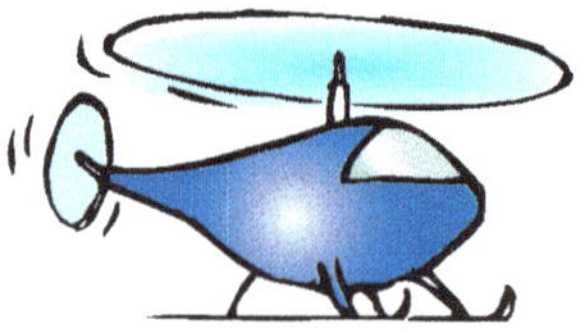

9

10

11

12

Associating initial sounds with letters: **c, d, g, h, n, p**

Name

Name each picture.
Circle the word that begins with the same sound.
Print the first letter to finish the picture name.

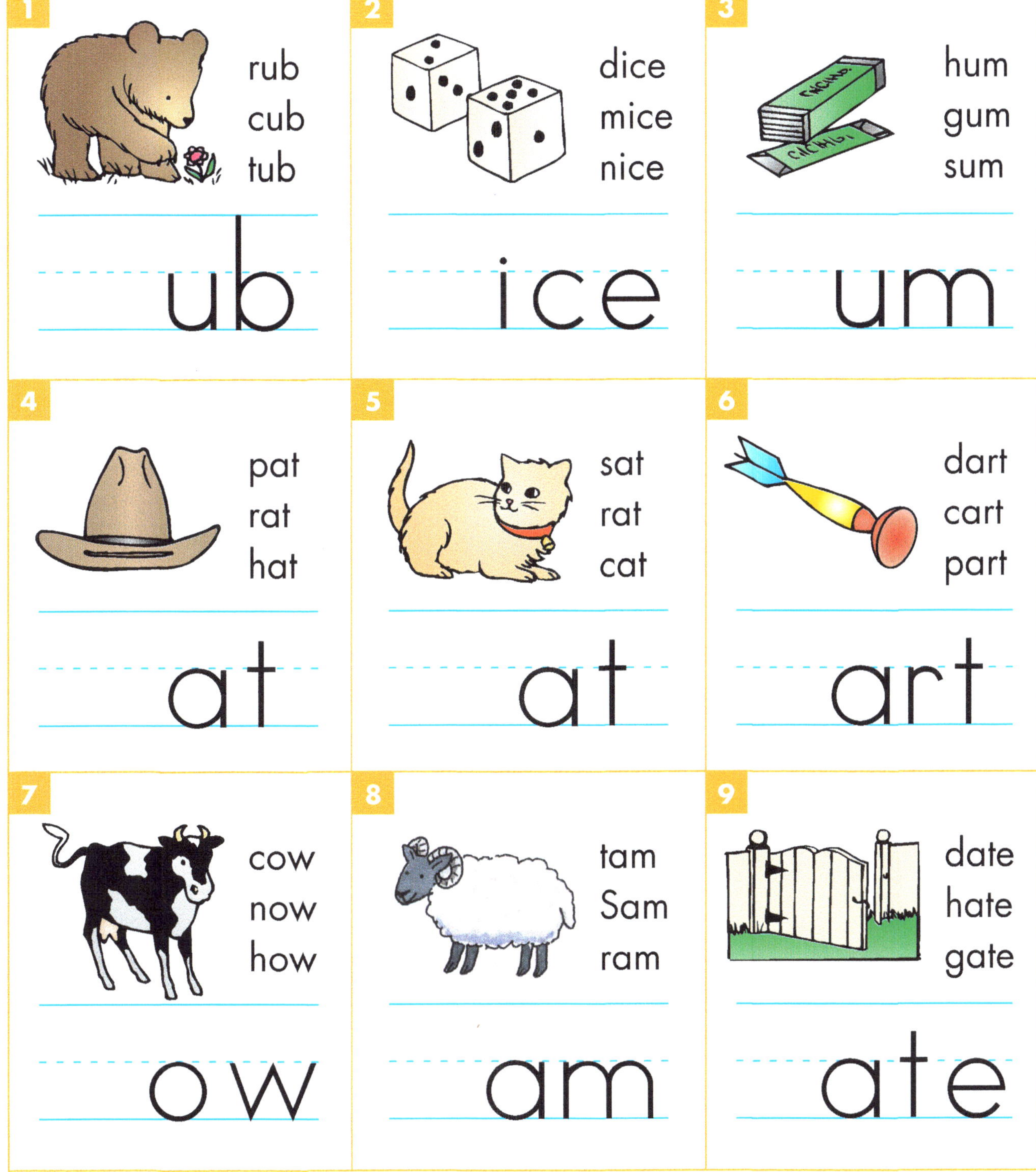

© Continental Press

Read the phrases.
Circle the phrase that goes with each picture.
Print the phrase under each picture.

a nap on a mat

a man in a cab

a cat in a hat

a big fan

a sad pig

Name ______________________

Oscar begins with the short **o** sound.
F**o**x has the short **o** sound in the middle.

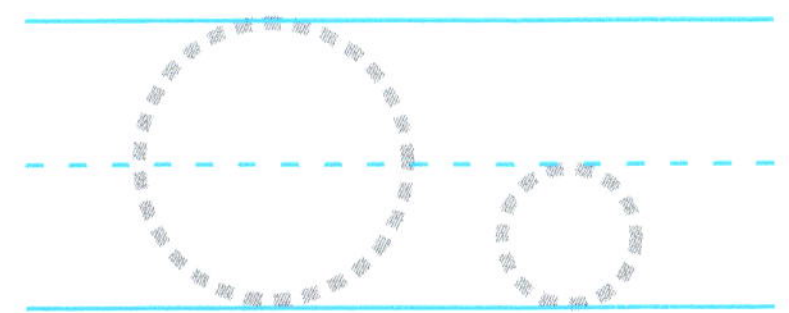

This is **O**scar the f**o**x.

Name each picture. Circle the picture if you hear the short **o** sound at the beginning or in the middle.

© Continental Press

Name each picture.
Print o if you hear the short **o** sound in the middle.

1	2	3
m ___ m	c ___ t	b ___ x

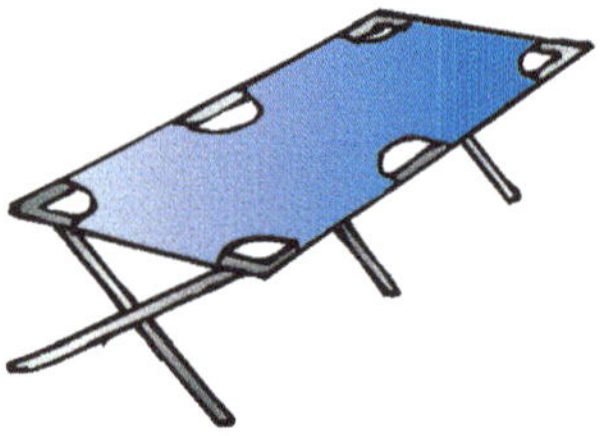

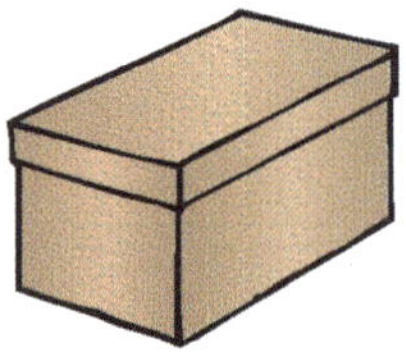

4	5	6
r ___ g	t ___ p	s ___ ck

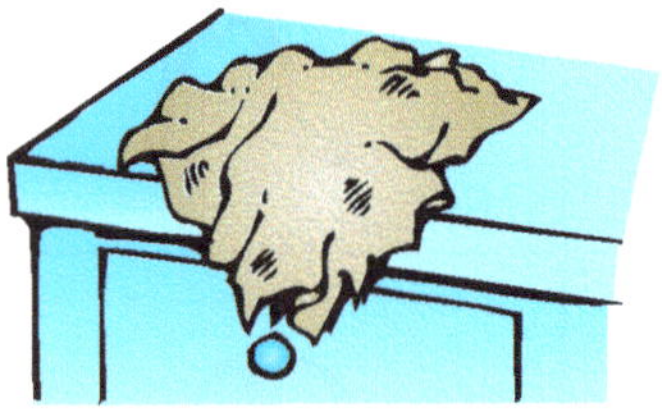

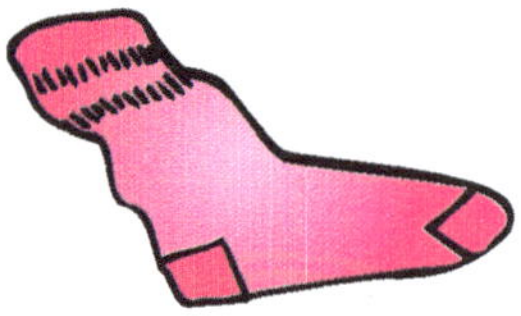

7	8	9
f ___ x	b ___ d	p ___ t

Name

Say the sound for the first letter.
Blend it with –**op.**
Print the word you say on the line.
Draw a line to the picture for the word.

m op

t op

h op

p op

© Continental Press

hot

hog

Name each picture.
Print ot or og to complete each picture name.

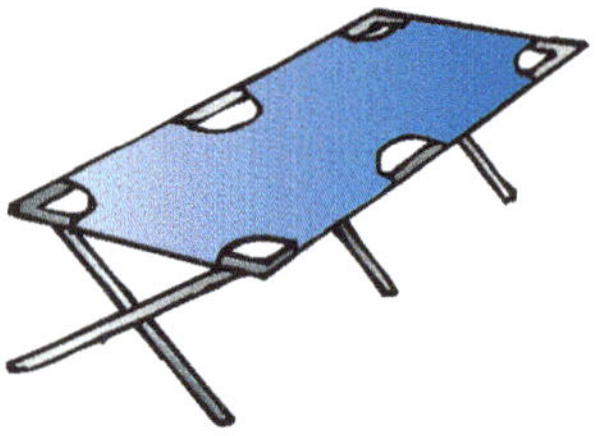

c  j  p

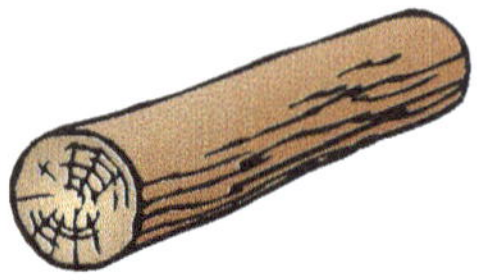

l i d fr

Name

Emma begins with the short **e** sound.
H**e**n has the short **e** sound in the middle.

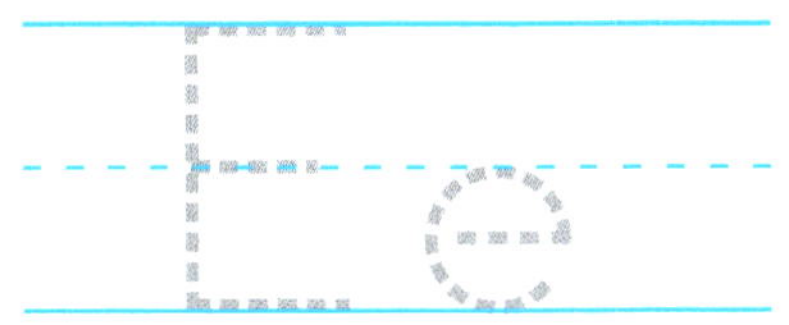

This is **E**mma the h**e**n.

Name each picture. Circle the picture if you hear the short **e** sound at the beginning or in the middle.

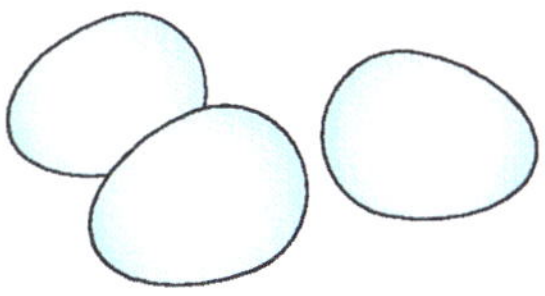

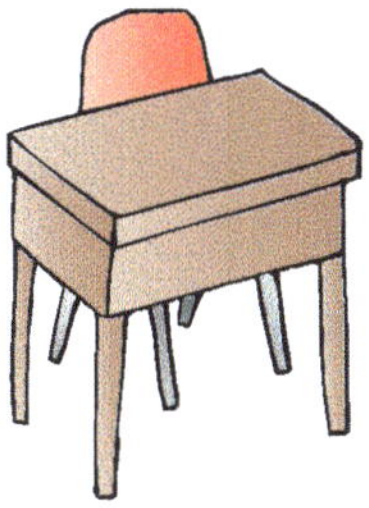

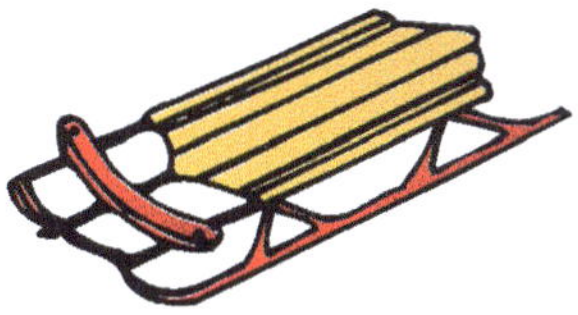

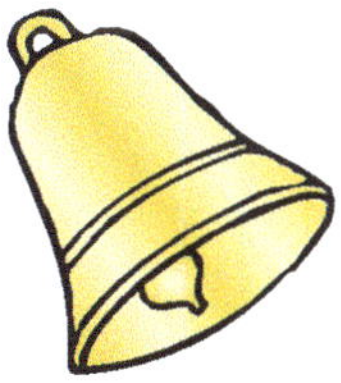

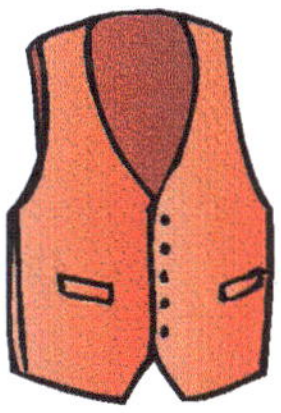

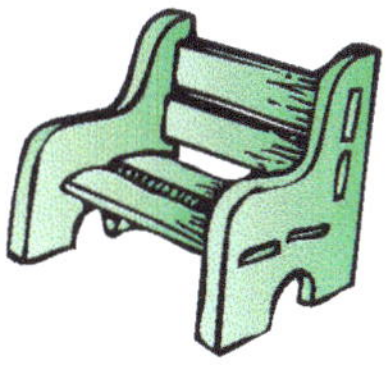

© Continental Press

Name each picture.
Print e if you hear the short **e** sound in the middle.

1 r _ d	2 t _ g	3 l _ g
4 b _ d	5 m _ n	6 w _ b
7 t _ nt	8 p _ t	9 n _ t

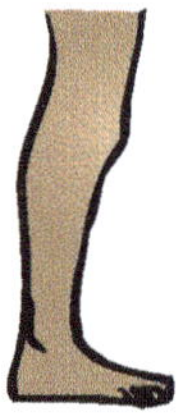

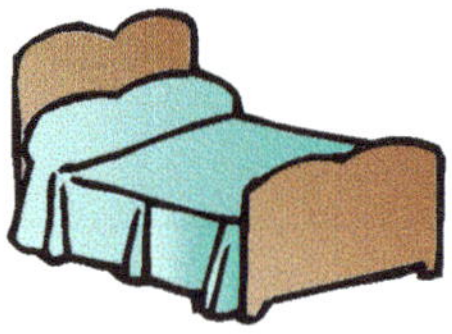

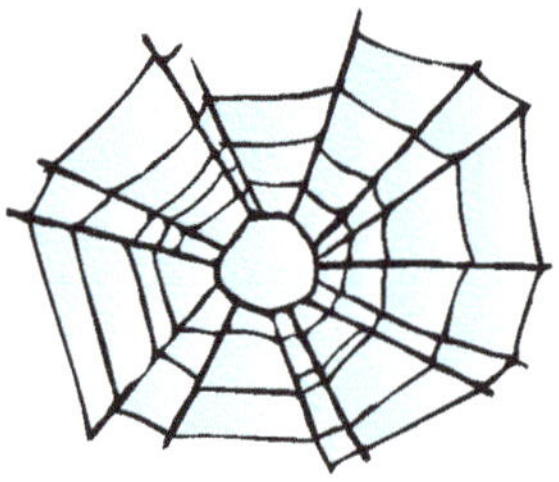

Name

Say the sound for the first letter.
Blend it with **–en**.
Print the word you say on the line.
Draw a line to the picture for the word.

© *Continental Press*

wet

beg

Name each picture.
Print et or eg to complete each picture name.

v

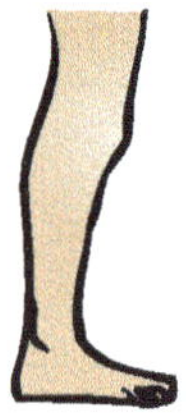

l

p

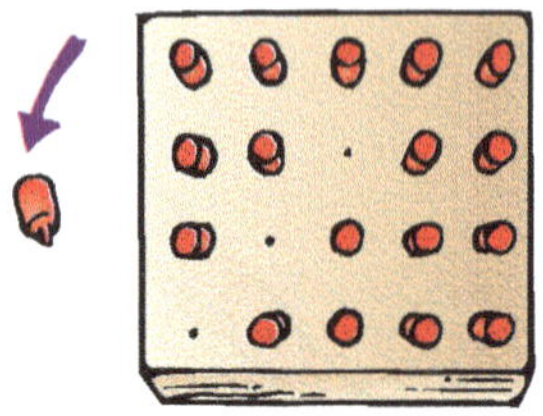

p

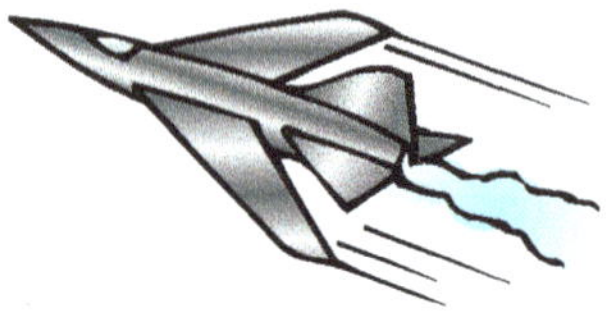

j

n

Name

Name each picture. Look at the words beside the picture.
Circle the word with the same middle sound.
Print the word on the lines below the picture.

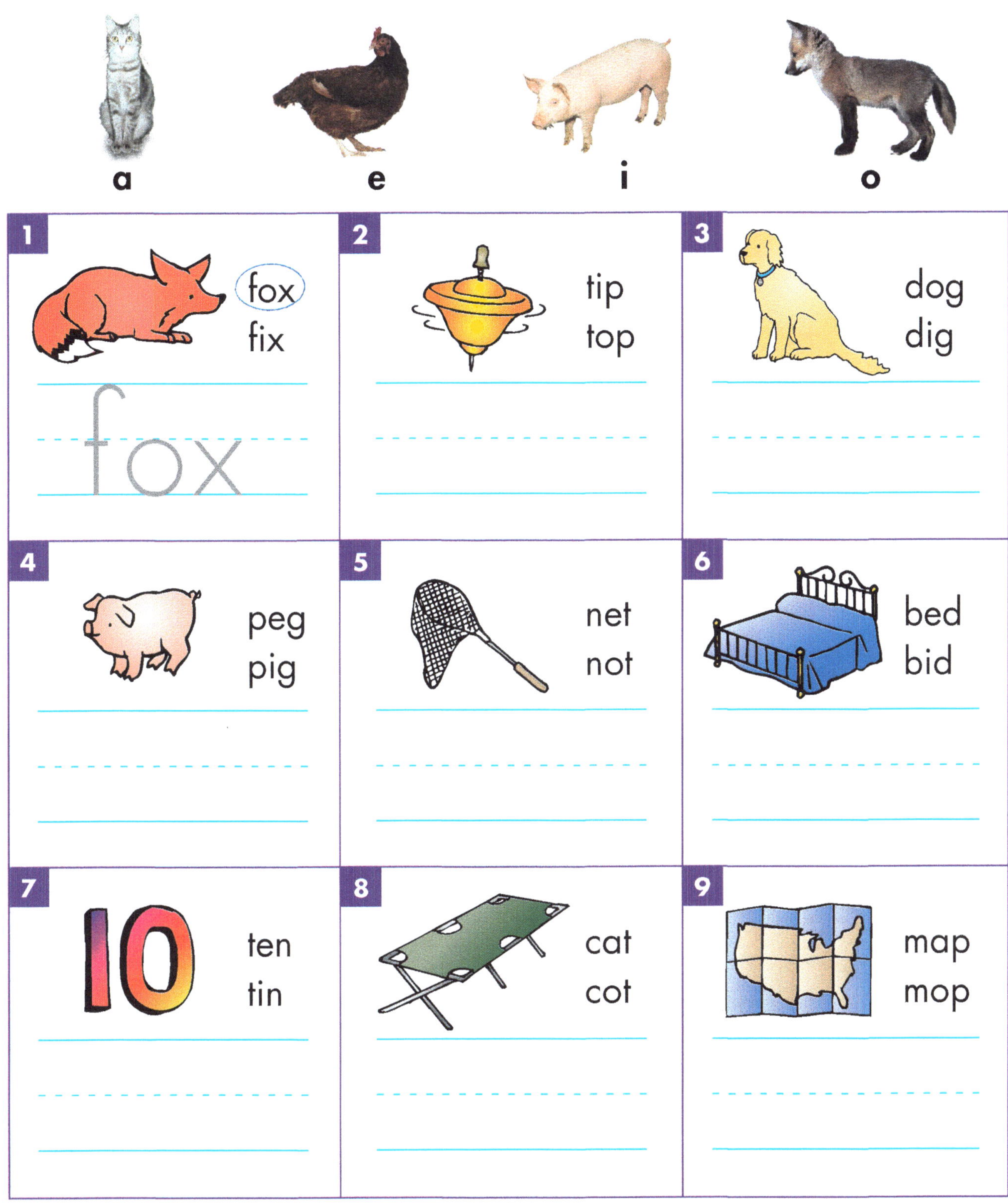

© Continental Press

Name each picture.
Circle the letter for the sound at the end of the word.
Print the letter to complete the word.

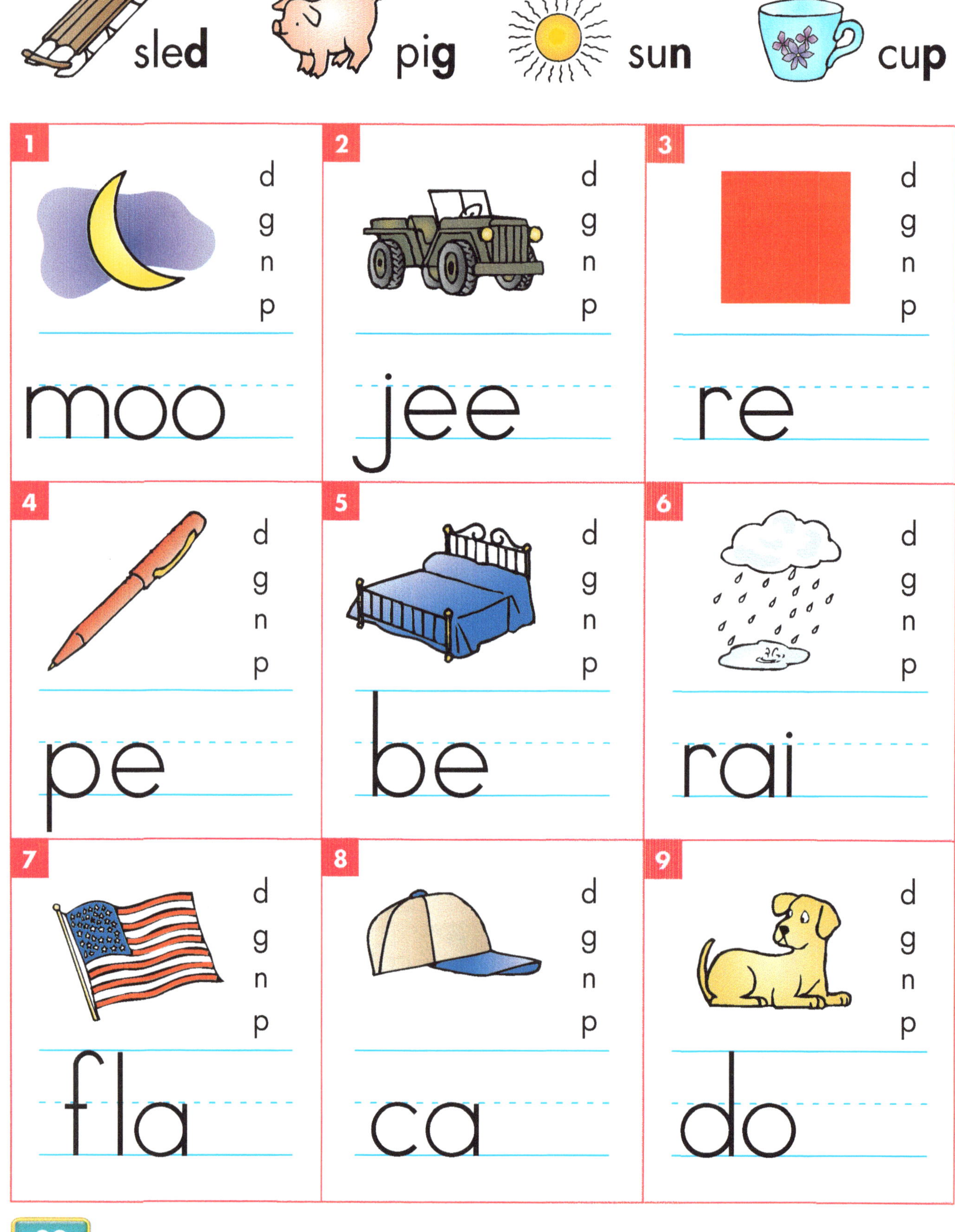

Name

Read each word. Draw a line to its picture.
Print the word beside the picture.

men

dog

bed

top

net

© Continental Press

Read the phrases.
Circle the phrase that goes with each picture.
Print the phrase under each picture.

a red cab

a hat in a can

a nap on a mat

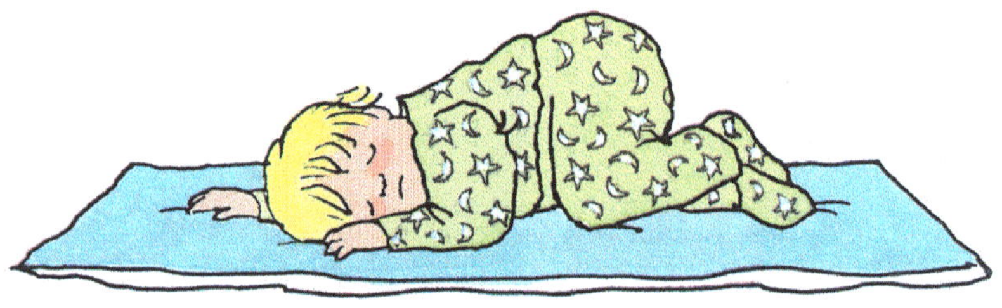

a hen in a pen

a pet in a net

a pot that is hot

the top of a mop

Ten Big Ants

1

Ten big ants hid in a pot.

3

6 Ten big ants hop on a bag.

8 Lots of ants can get fed!

fold

cut

© Continental Press

2 Ten big ants sat on the mat.

Ten big ants rip the top. 7

4 Ten big ants got in a can.

Ten big ants can go in! 5

Unit 3
Progress Check

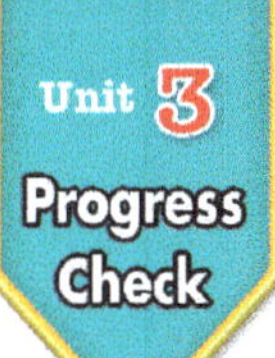

Name ______________________________

Listen to the name of each picture.
Circle the letter for its beginning sound.

1 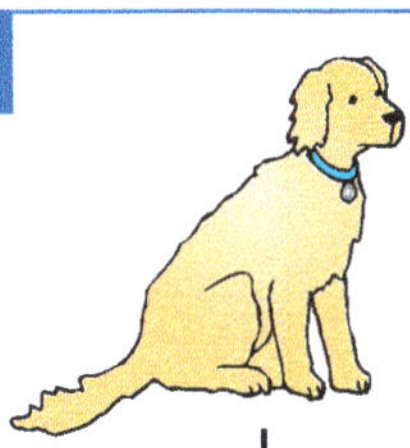 h d n

2 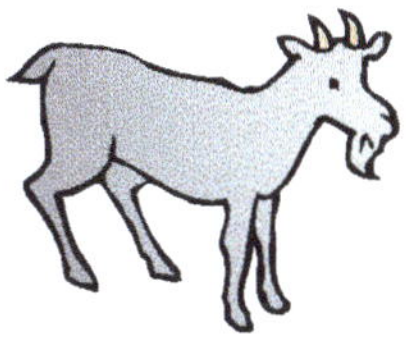 g d t

3 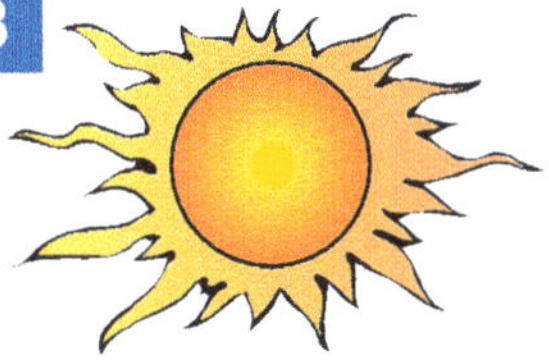 f g s

4 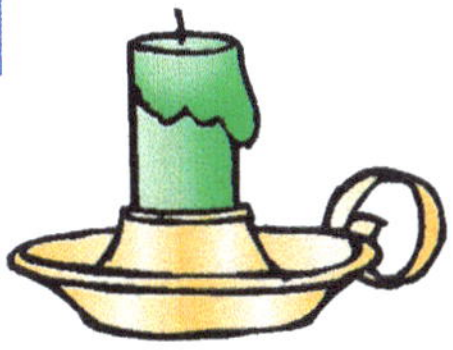 r b c

5 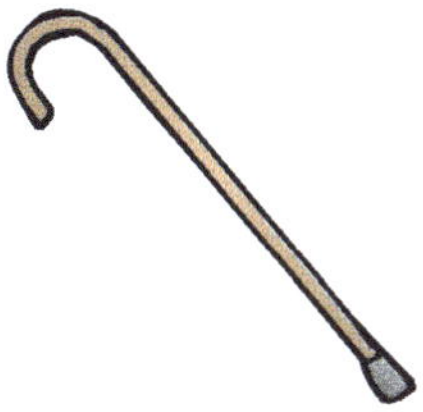 s r c

6 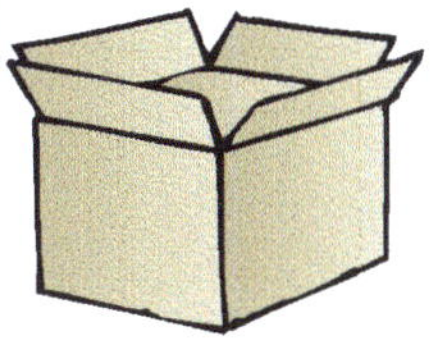 d b h

7 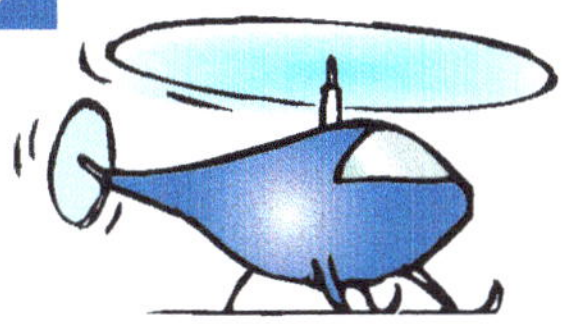 h m d

8 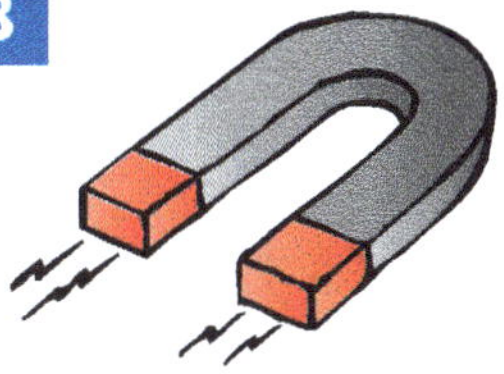 n m r

9 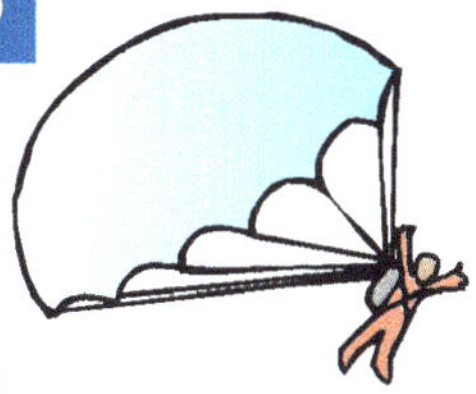 b p g

10 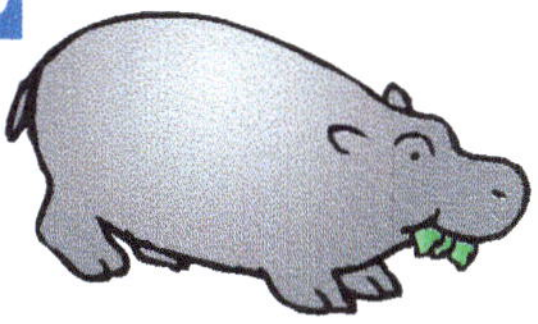 h r m

11 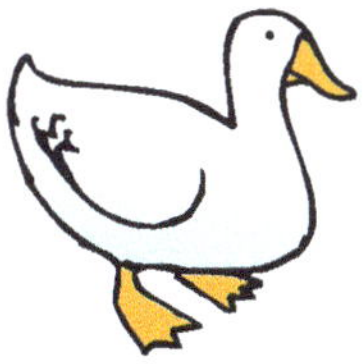 p s d

12 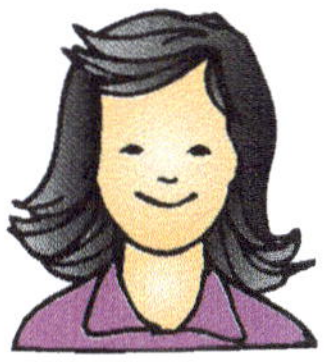 r g h

13 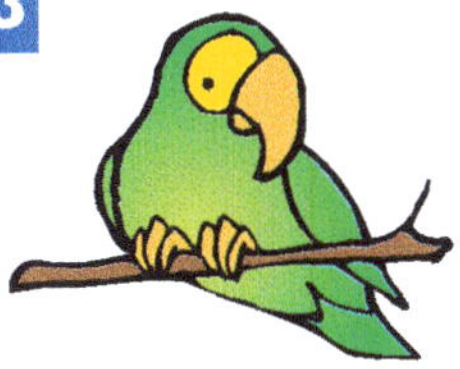 c p d

14 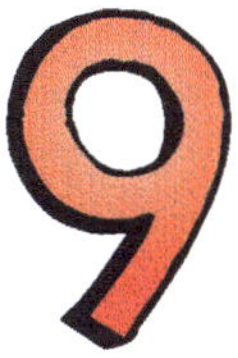

n f m

15 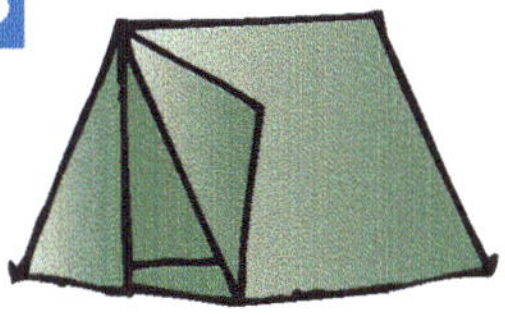 r t s

16 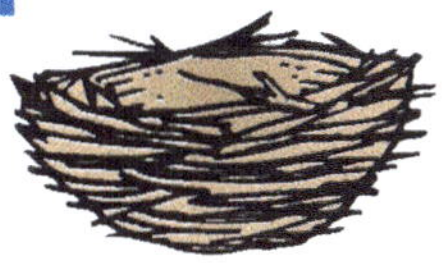 h n b

17 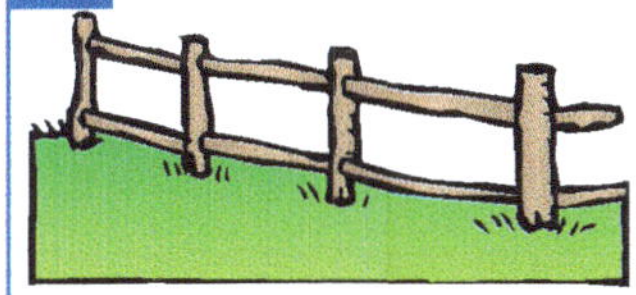 d s f

18 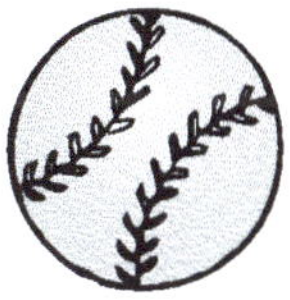 b r g

19 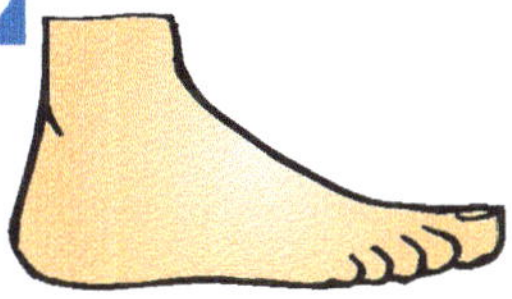 f p s

20 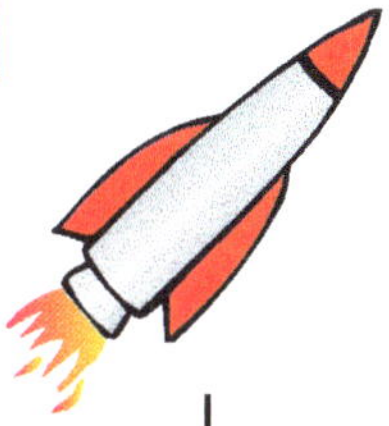 n h r

© Continental Press

Listen to each word.
Find the word in the box and circle it.

1	2	3	4	5
hen pin pen pet	get gob pot got	it on in at	dog dig dip big	pig pen beg peg

6	7	8	9	10
nod not cod Ned	den deb din hen	fob fig bog fog	bad had hat hid	cab nab cap cob

11	12	13	14	15
hop dog hog hip	bat cot cat can	sit sip nip sap	nag nog bag nap	top sip tin tip

Chums

He sits and begs; he gives a paw;
He is, as you can see,
The finest dog you ever saw,
And he belongs to me.

He follows everywhere I go
And even when I swim.
I laugh because he thinks, you know,
That I belong to him.

Arthur Guiterman

d

Dear Family,

Our class is now learning the sounds for the letters **j, k, l, qu, v, w, y,** and **z,** and many words that begin with those sounds. Then we will add another vowel sound, short **u** (bug). We will also be learning about the sound of **x** at the end of words (fox). As we learn to combine these sounds, your child will be able to read more words and some basic stories.

Here are a few ways that you can help your child at home.

- When your child brings home a booklet such as the story "Ten Big Ants," take time to listen and read along. Your praise and interest will help your child become an eager reader.
- Make the sound of any of the letters above, and have your child write the letter or letters. (The letters **q** and **u** are written together to represent the sound /kw/.) Then add letters to make a word. (qu→iz)
- Read the poem on the other side of this page aloud. If you have a pet or pets at home, talk about how the dog in this poem is the same or different from them. Your child may be able to read some of the words in the poem.
- There are many poems written about pets and animals. You may enjoy reading some of these with your child. *Feathered Ones and Furry* by Aileen Fisher is a book of poetry about animals. In *My Father's Hands* by Joanne Ryder, readers are introduced to small creatures in a garden.

Name

Jolly **j**uggler begins with the sound /j/.
We print the letter j for the sound /j/.
Lazy **l**ion begins with the sound /l/.
We print the letter l for the sound /l/.

Name each picture. Print the letter it begins with – j or l.

© Continental Press

Name each picture.
Find the word that begins with the same sound.
Circle the word and print it.

Associating initial sounds with letters in words: **d, j, l, s**

Name

Katy **k**angaroo begins with the sound /k/.
We print the letter k for the sound /k/.
Volcano begins with the sound /v/.
We print the letter v for the sound /v/.

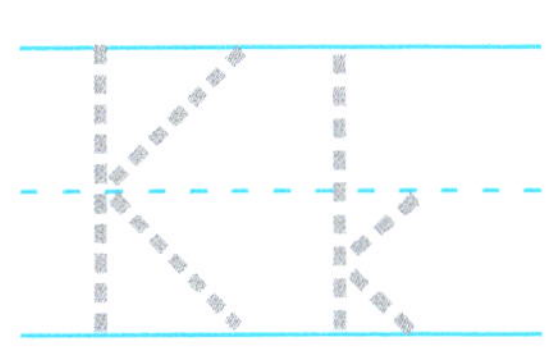

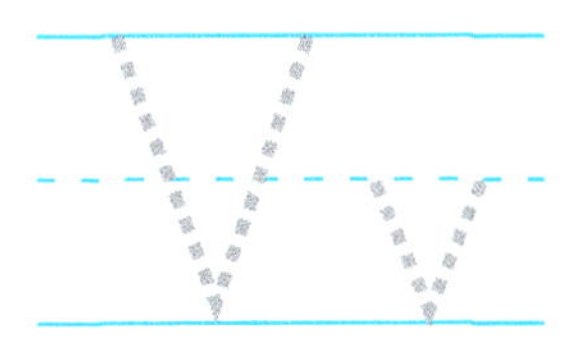

Name each picture. Print the letter it begins with – k or v.

© Continental Press

Name each picture.
Find the word that begins with the same sound.
Circle the word and print it.

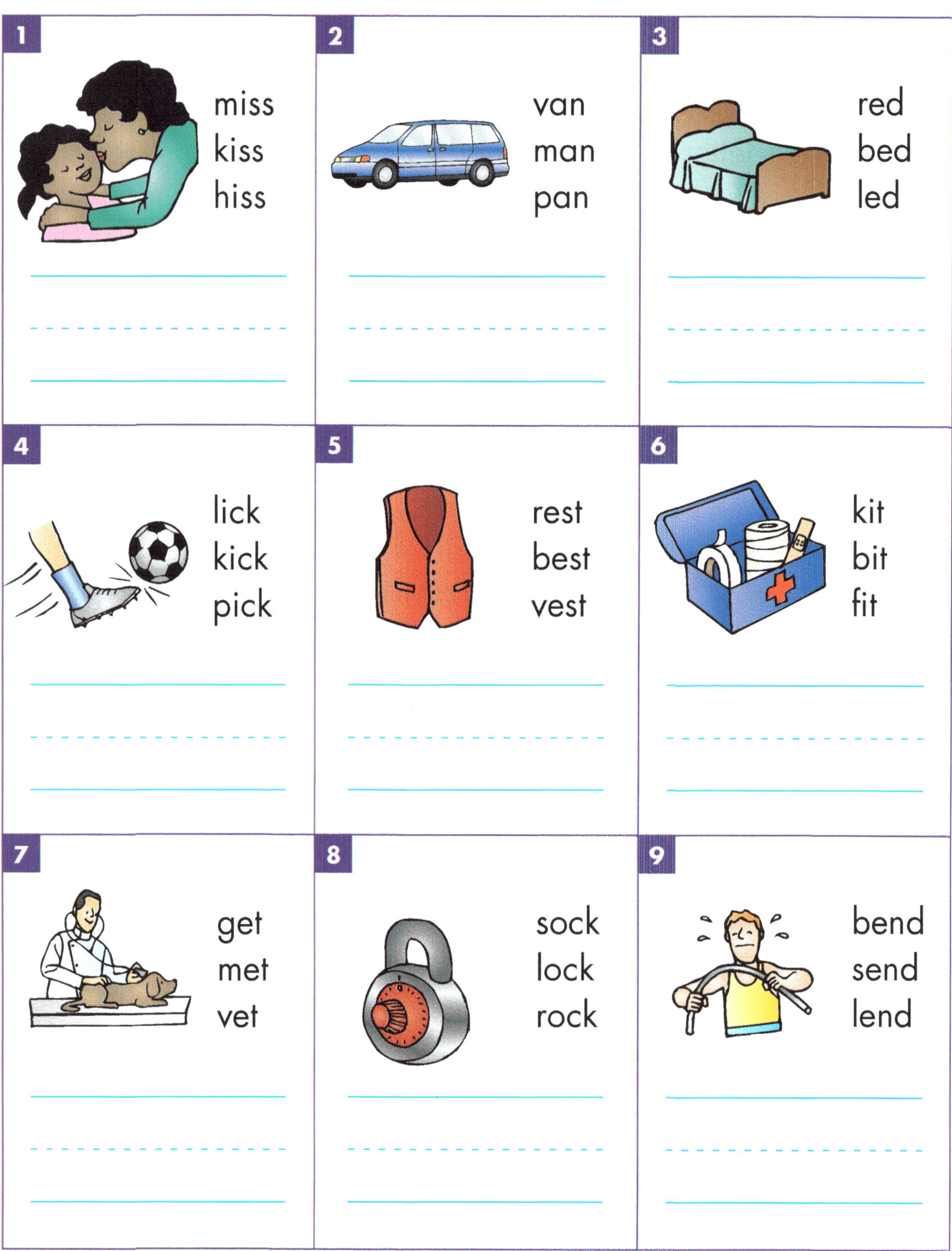

 Associating initial sounds with letters in words: **b, k, l, v**

Name

Wiggly **w**orm begins with the sound /w/.
We print the letter w for the sound /w/.
Zany **z**ebra begins with the sound /z/.
We print the letter z for the sound /z/.

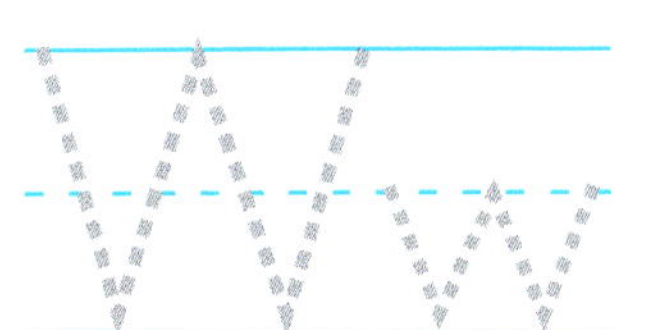

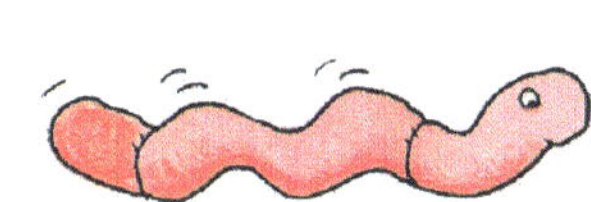

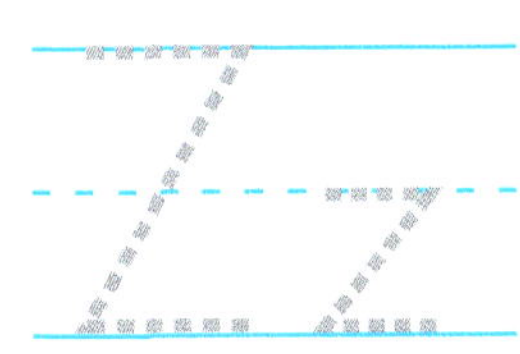

Name each picture. Print the letter it begins with – w or z.

© Continental Press

Name the letter and the pictures in each row.
If the picture name begins with the sound of the letter,
fill in the circle under the picture.

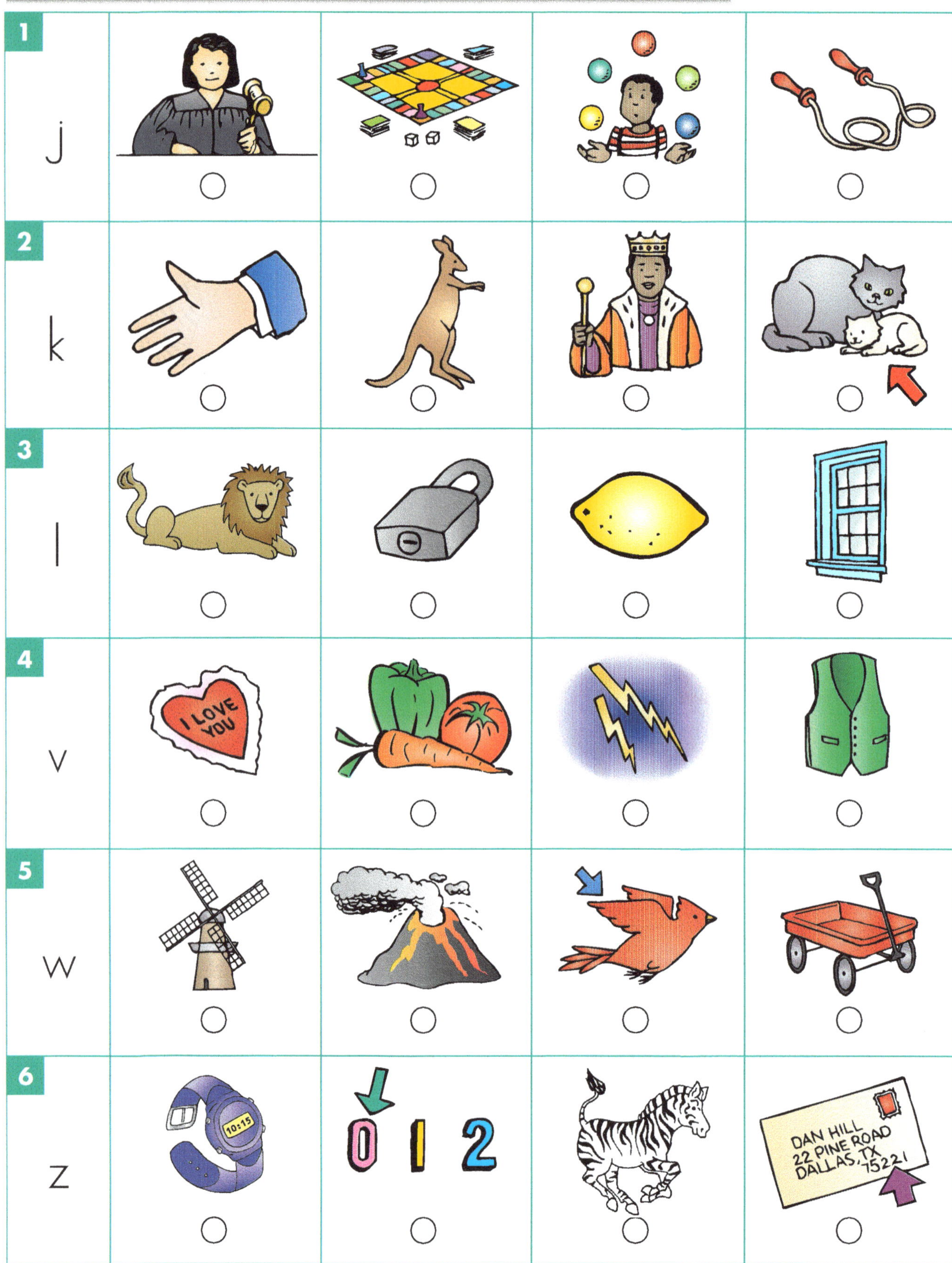

Review initial consonants: **j, k, l, v, w, z**

Name ____________________

Name each picture.
Find the word that begins with the same sound.
Circle the word and print it.

© Continental Press

Associating initial sounds with letters in words: **m, r, w, z**

Read the phrases.
Circle the phrase that goes with each picture.
Print the phrase under each picture.

a frog on a log

a tan jet

a wet hat

a web in the den

a pin in the kit

a bed for a cat

a dog in a van

Name

Ug begins with the short **u** sound.
B**u**g has the short **u** sound in the middle.

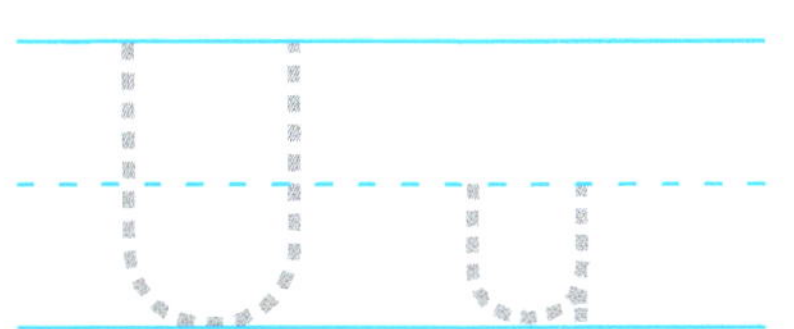

This is **U**g the b**u**g.

Name each picture. Circle the picture if you hear the short **u** sound at the beginning or in the middle.

© *Continental Press*

Name each picture.
Print u if you hear the short **u** sound in the middle.

1  b d

2 h t

3 p p

4 t b

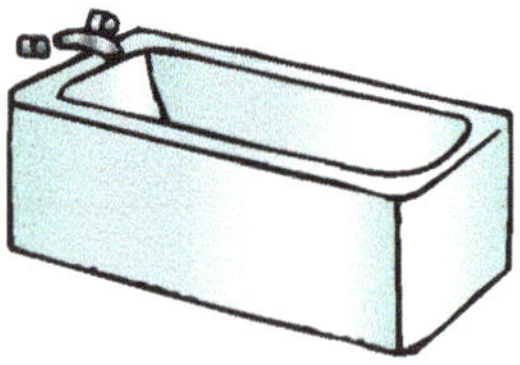

5 g m

6 c n

7 c p

8 n t

9 b s

Name

Say the sound for the first letter.
Blend it with –**ug**.
Print the word you say on the line.
Draw a line to the picture for the word.

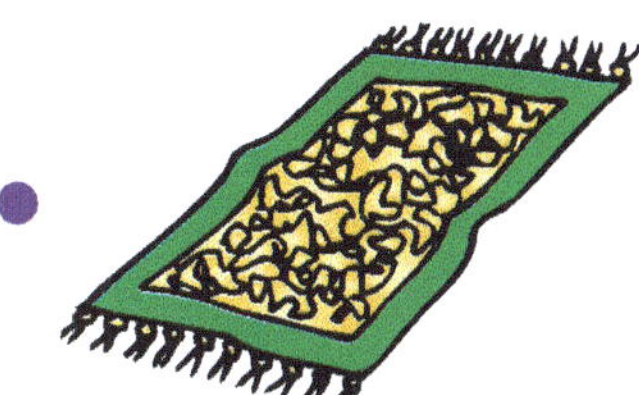

© Continental Press

sub

sun

cut

Name each picture.
Print ub, un, or ut to complete each picture name.

c

b

r

h

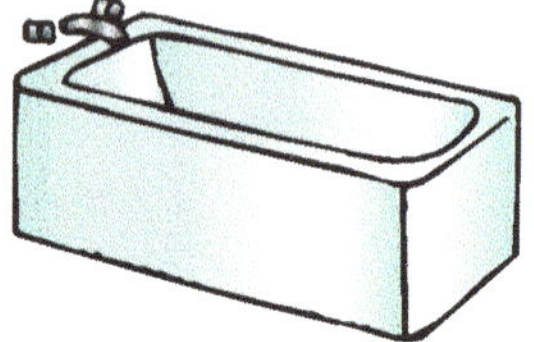

t

n

Name

Name each picture. Look at the words beside the picture.
Circle the word with the same middle sound.
Print the word on the lines below the picture.

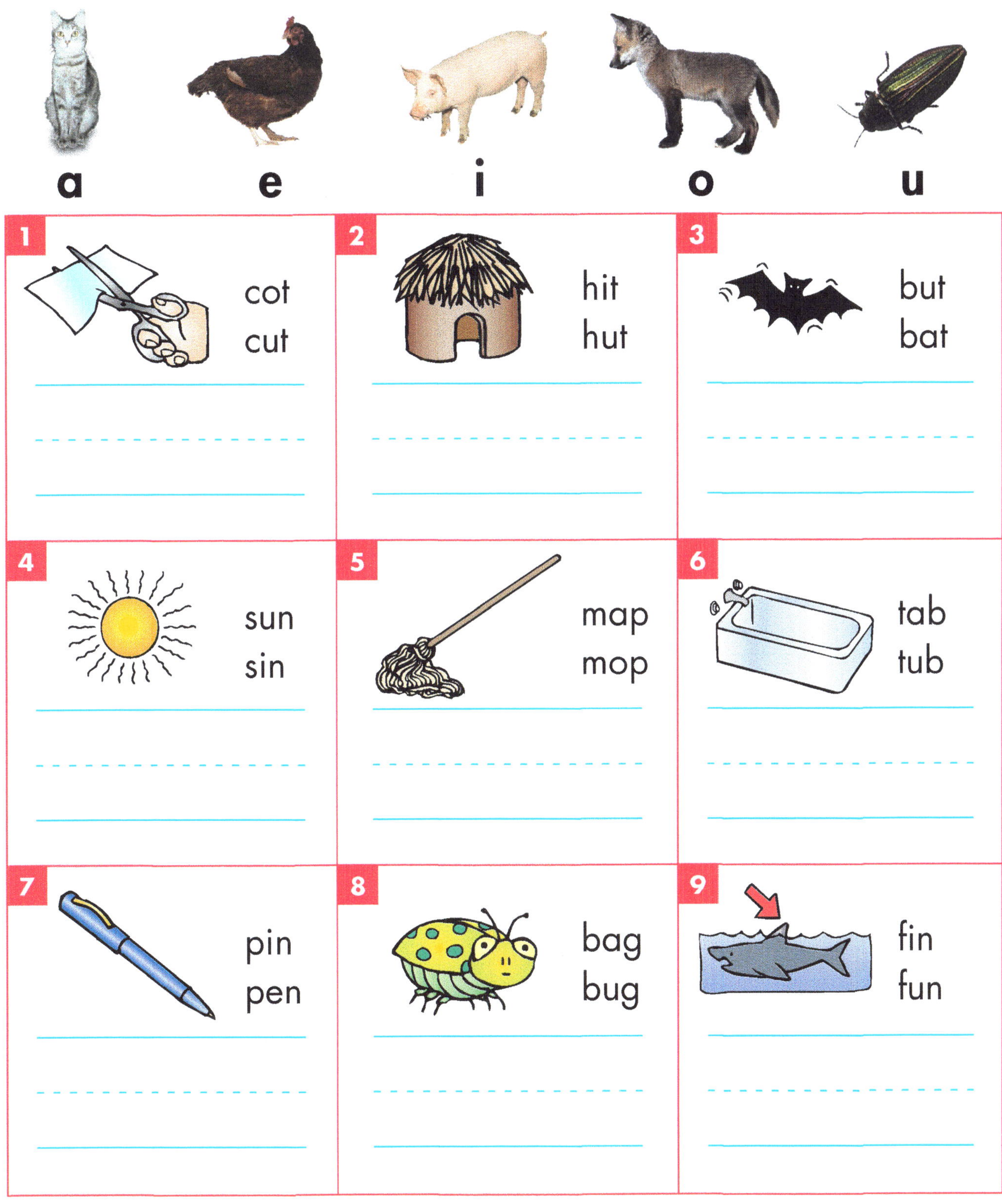

© Continental Press

Name each picture.
Circle the letter for the sound at the end of the word.
Print the letter to complete the word.

Associating final sounds with letters in words: **f, l, r, s, x**

Name

Read each word. Draw a line to its picture.
Print the word beside the picture.

gas

fox

six

bus

web

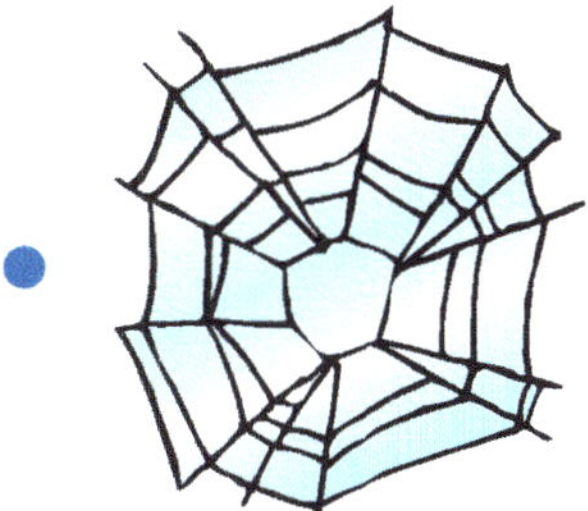

© Continental Press

Read the phrases.
Circle the phrase that goes with each picture.
Print the phrase under each picture.

a hug for mom

on top of the jet

a spot on the rug

bug on a bud

cub in a box

a run in the sun

a big red mug

Name

Quiet **q**ueen begins with the sound /kw/.
We print the letters qu for the sound /kw/.
Yo-**y**o begins with the sound /y/.
We print the letter y for the sound /y/.

Name each picture. Print the letter or letters it begins with – qu or y.

© Continental Press

Name each picture.
Find the word that begins with the same sound.
Circle the word and print it.

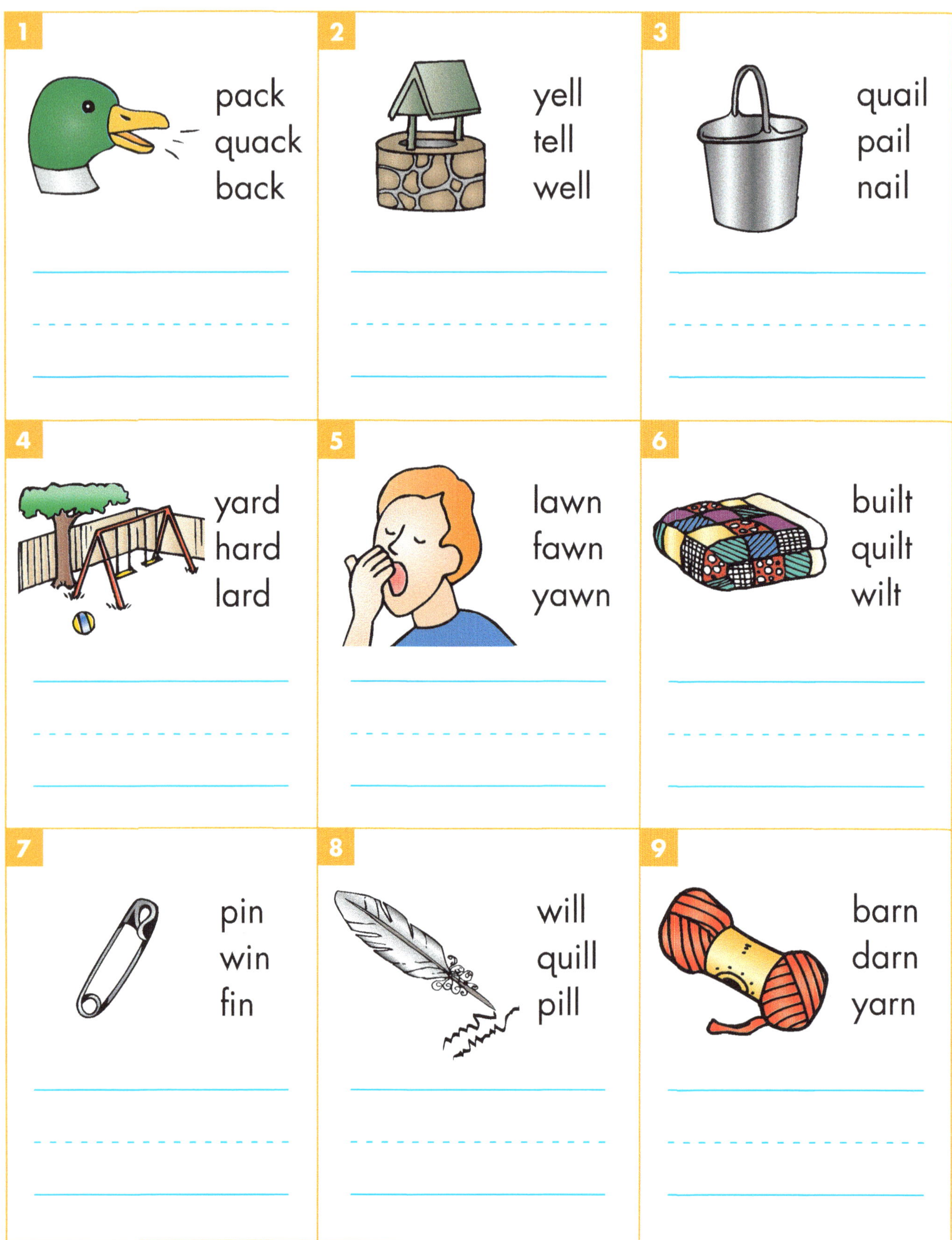

 Associating initial sounds with letters in words: **p, qu, w, y**

Name

The titles of books in a library are in alphabetical order, starting with **A.**
The words in the box are the missing titles.
Print them on the lines, in alphabetical order.

Fox	Eggs	Cats	Hill	Kits	Bats	Jets

1. Ants
2.
3.
4. Dogs
5.
6.
7. Grass
8.
9. Insects
10.
11.
12. Lamps
13. Mitts

© Continental Press

Here are more book titles in a library.
They are in alphabetical order, starting with **N.**
The words in the box are the missing titles.
Print them on the lines, in alphabetical order.

Sun	Oxen	Up	Yaks	Pets	Webs

1. Nuts
2.
3.
4. Quilts
5. Rams
6.
7. TV
8.
9. Vets
10.
11. X-rays
12.
13. Zoo

8 What do you think will happen next? Finish the story.

1

fold

6 "Now look!" said Kim. "It is too wet to go."

"Come, Rex and Zip," said Kim, "We must go to the vet." 3

© Continental Press

2 Kim has a big dog and a little cat.

“We will not go to the vet, yet.” 7

4 Rex and Zip run and jump.
They will not quit.

“Sit, Rex, sit!” Kim said.
“Stop that, Zip!” 5

Unit 4 Progress Check

Name ______________________

Listen to the name of each picture.
Circle the letter for its beginning sound.

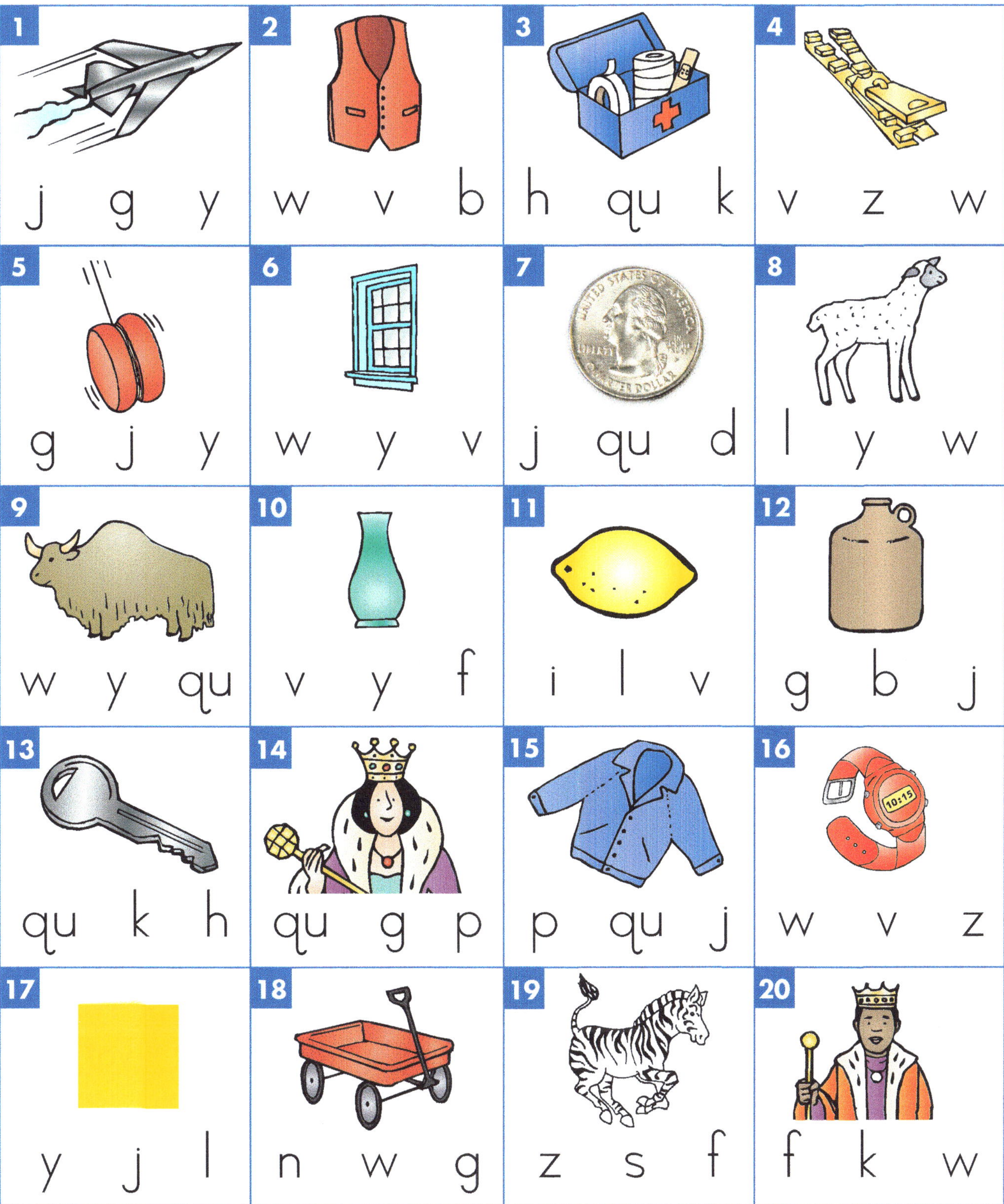

© Continental Press

Unit 4 Progress Check

Listen to each word.
Find the word in the box and circle it.

1	2	3	4	5
yet bet met vet	bun bin pen pun	lot lip hip hot	fan van fat vat	deb web wed bed
6	**7**	**8**	**9**	**10**
had fix fox fad	rut rot but bib	jab bag bug jug	kid hit kit hid	bus bud bat buzz
11	**12**	**13**	**14**	**15**
job cob jig cop	quip cut quit kit	mop zip map zap	will wit mitt mill	yam van vat yum

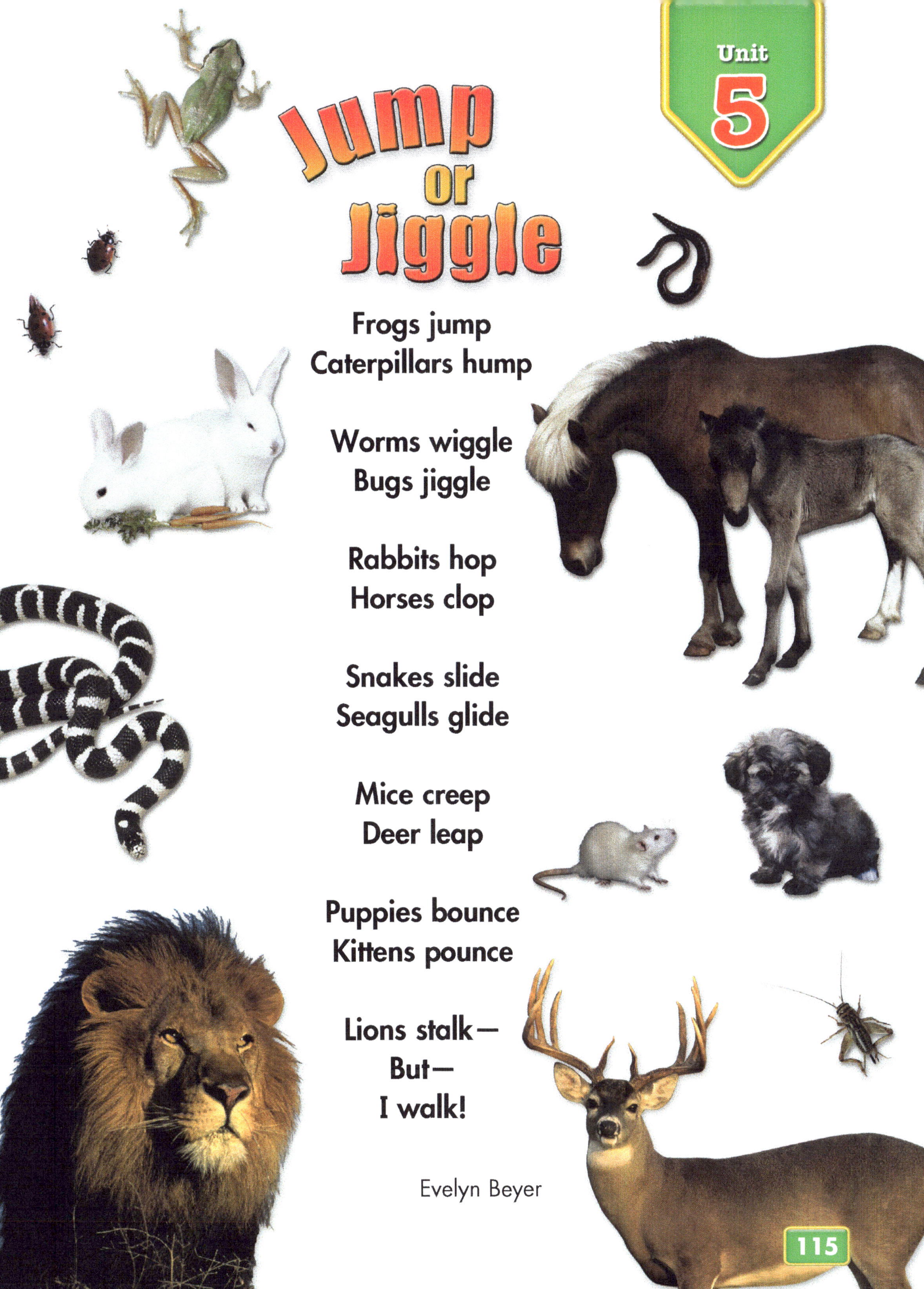

Jump or Jiggle

Frogs jump
Caterpillars hump

Worms wiggle
Bugs jiggle

Rabbits hop
Horses clop

Snakes slide
Seagulls glide

Mice creep
Deer leap

Puppies bounce
Kittens pounce

Lions stalk—
But—
I walk!

Evelyn Beyer

Dear Family,

Your child is gaining experience in learning letters and the sounds they stand for. Now we are going to begin reading words with letter combinations, such as those in **child** and in **think.** We will be learning longer words and words with special endings, too.

Here are some ways to share what our class will be doing with your child.

- Listen to your child read books and take-home booklets such as "Kim's Pets." If your child gets "stuck" on a word, ask what sounds are in that word. Then help your child blend the sounds together and say the word.
- Look for food names that use letter combinations. Ask your child what two letters make the sound that they hear at the beginning or end of words such as **ch**eese, **cr**ackers, **fr**uit, **sp**aghetti, and fi**sh**.
- Read the poem on the other side of this page aloud. Have your child listen for animal names that begin with blends (**fr**ogs, **sn**akes). Then read the poem again, and listen for words with two or more parts (syllables)—caterpillars, wiggle, jiggle, rabbits, horses, seagulls, puppies, and kittens.
- Children often like stories about animals and animal babies.
- You might read *Rabbits and Raindrops* by Jim Arnosky to your child.

Name ______________________

Name each picture. Print the first two letters for the beginning blend.

Name each picture. Print the first two letters for the beginning blend.

br dr gr tr

Name

Name each picture. Print the first two letters for the beginning blend.

1

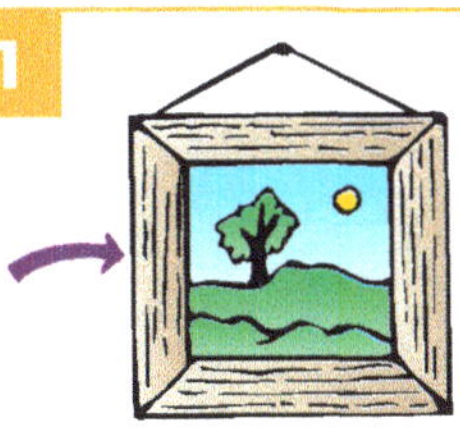

2

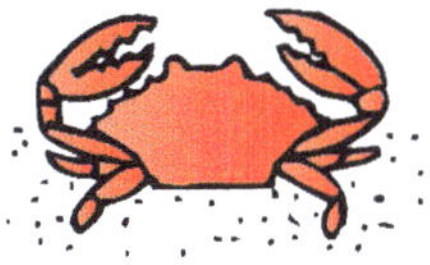

3

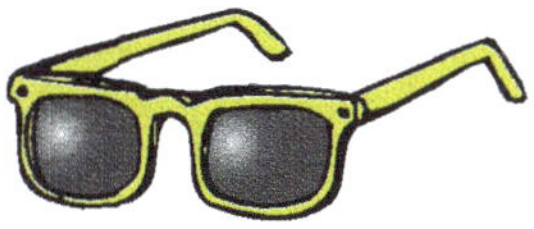

4

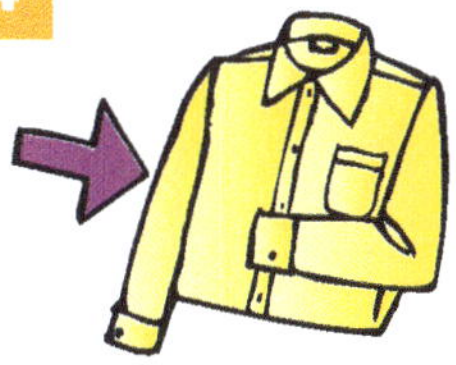

5

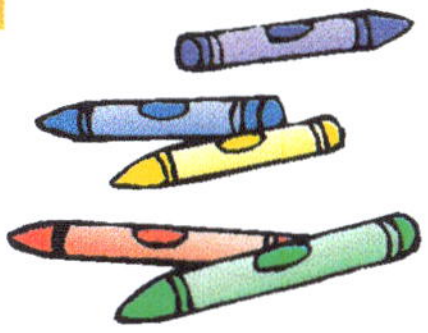

6

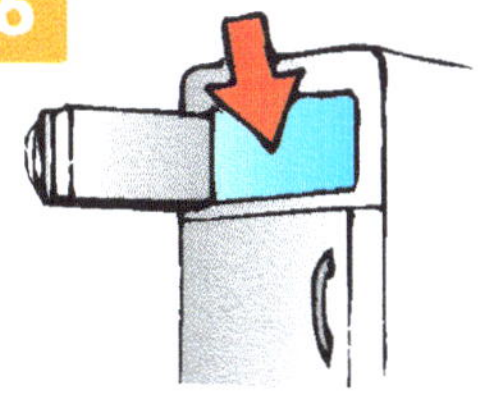

7

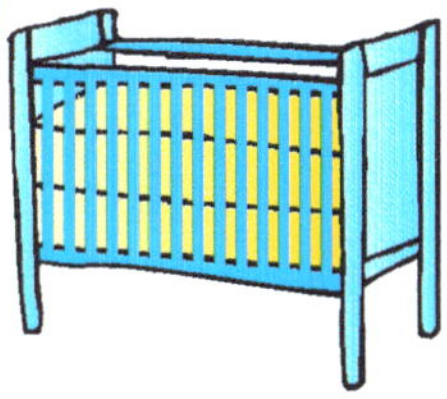

8

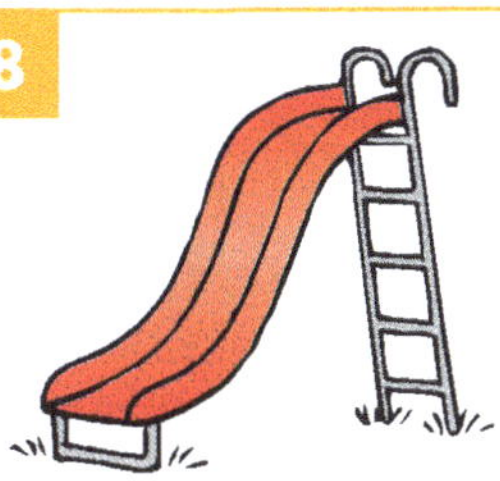

9

GLUE

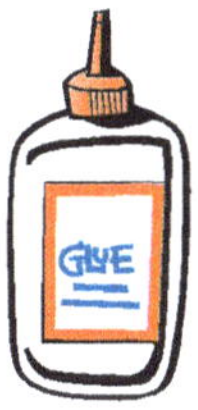

10

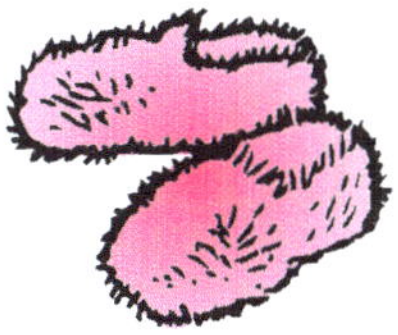

11

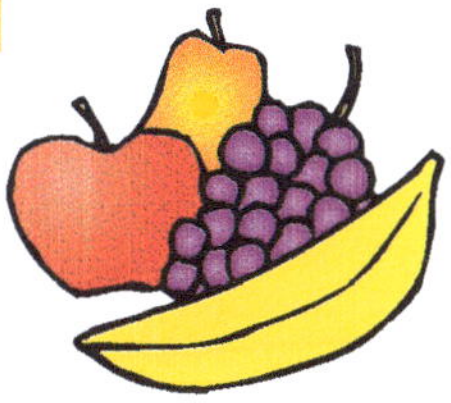

12

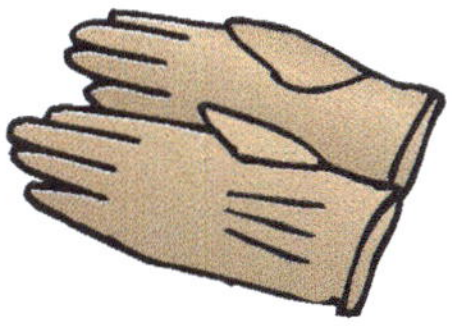

© Continental Press

Name each picture. Print the first two letters for the beginning blend.

Name

Read the phrases.
Circle the phrase that goes with each picture.
Print the phrase under each picture.

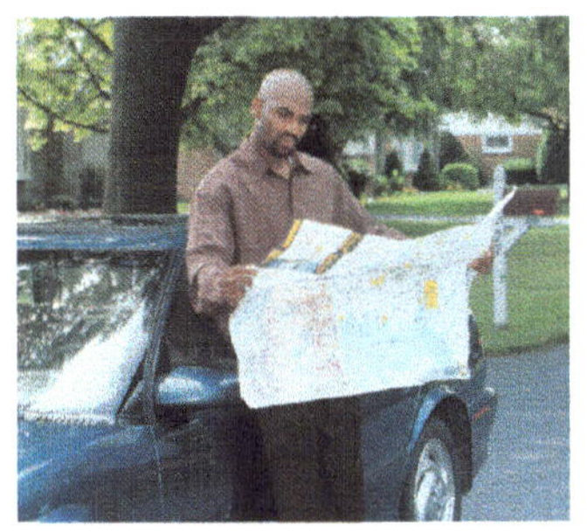

a plan for a trip

a frog in the mud

a crab in the trap

a flag and a drum

a sled and a crib

a drop in the cup

a swim in the tub

© Continental Press

Read the story. Circle the word that completes each sentence. Print the missing word in each sentence.

Fred had a __________ for his mom.	grant slant plant
He did not want to __________ it.	drop plop flop
But he did not see the __________ on the step.	slot spot stop
Fred did drop the plant, and he fell __________ !	slat blot flat
"That was not a good __________ ," he said.	trip drip clip

Name ______________________________

Some words end in **ck** or double letters.
The two letters together have the same sound as one letter.

du**ck** do**ll** gra**ss**

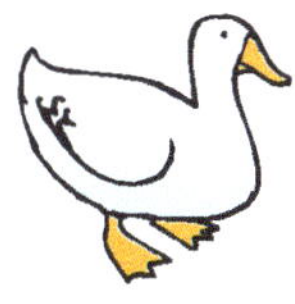

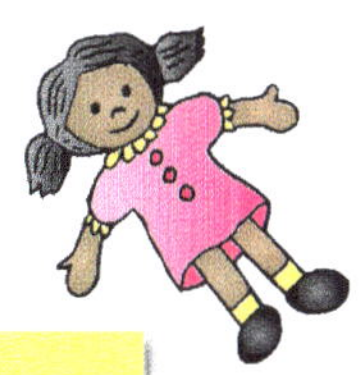

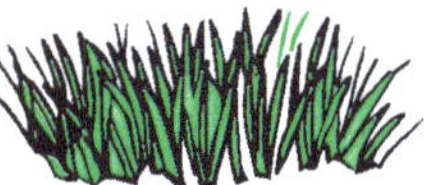

Circle the word that names the picture.

1 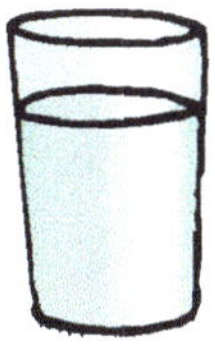
gas
glass
gull

2 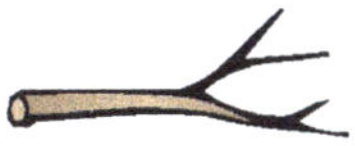
stick
still
stiff

3 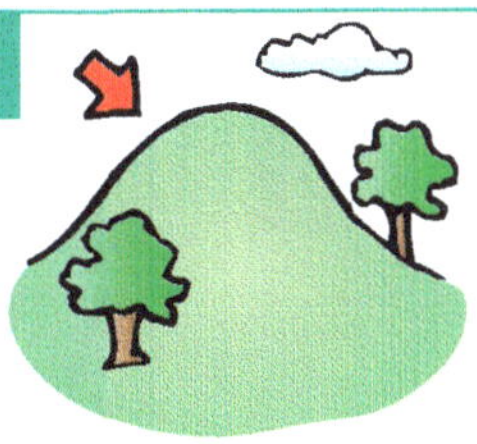
hill
hiss
hall

4 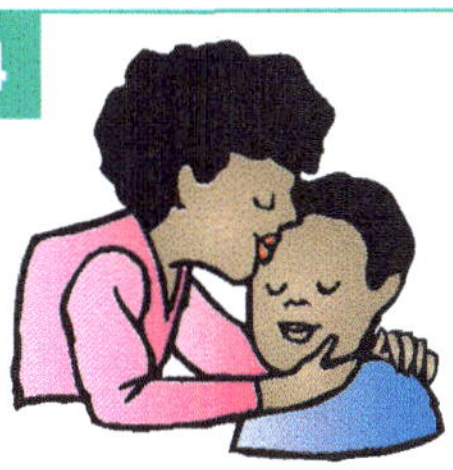
kit
kiss
kick

5 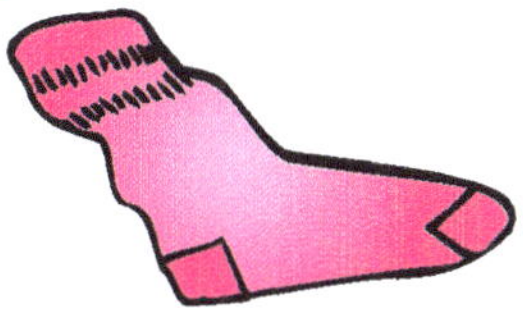
sell
sock
stuck

6 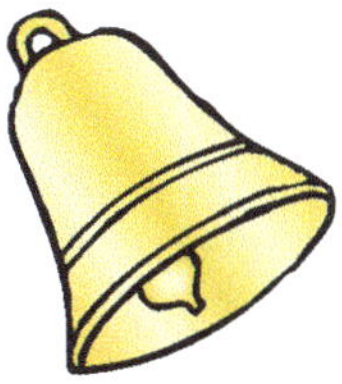
bell
best
deck

7 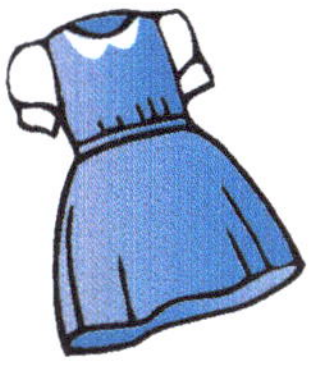
drill
dress
brick

8 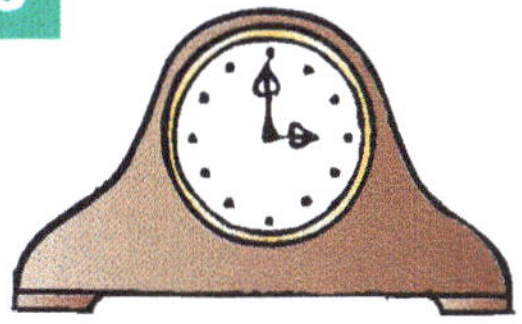
class
cluck
clock

9 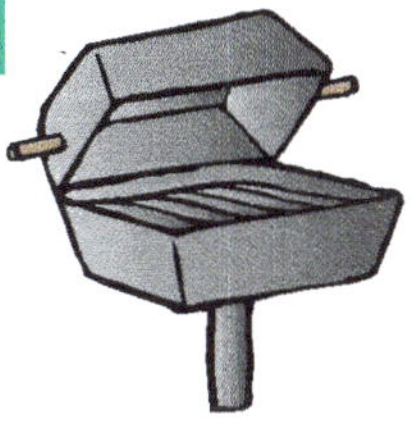
gruff
grass
grill

10 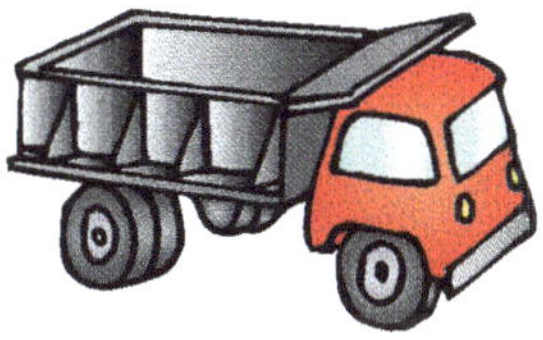
trunk
trill
truck

11 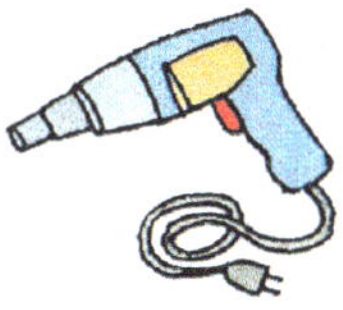
deck
drill
dress

12 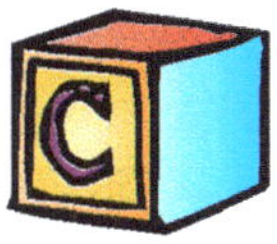

ball
back
block

© Continental Press

Some words end with blends.

ha**nd**

pi**nk**

a**nt**

la**mp**

ma**sk**

ve**st**

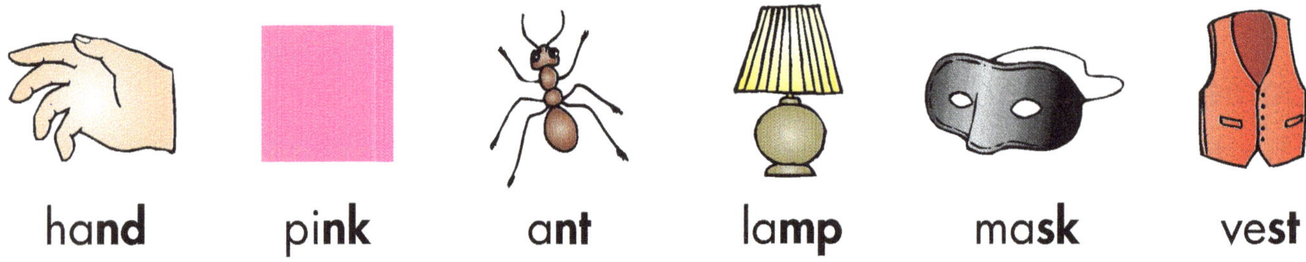

Name each picture. Listen for the sounds at the end of the word. Print the letters to complete the word.

1
tru

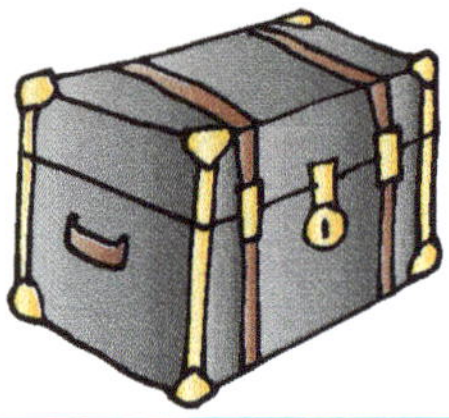

2
sa

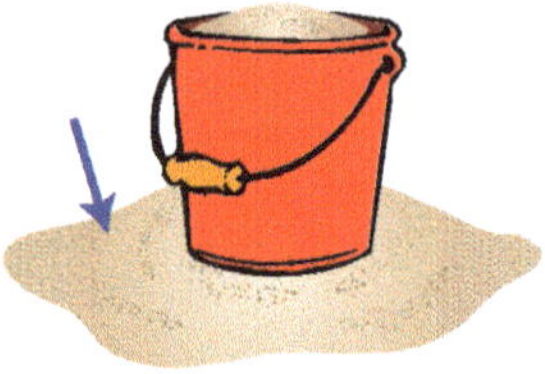

3
pla

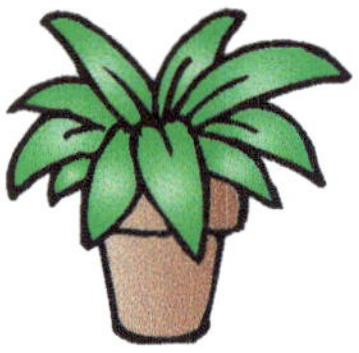

4
ne

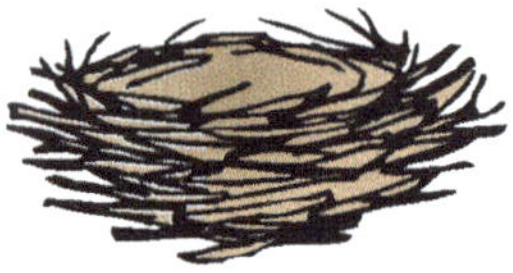

5
stu

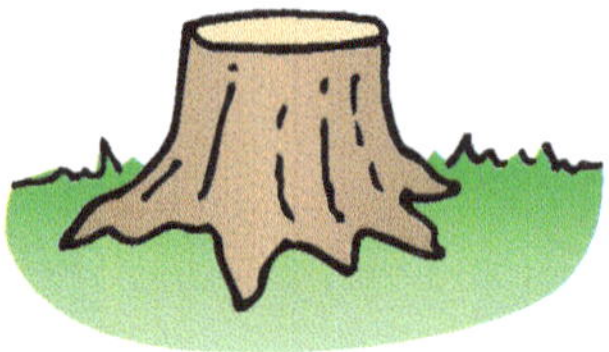

6
de

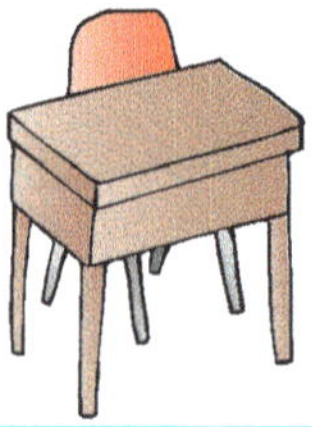

7
si

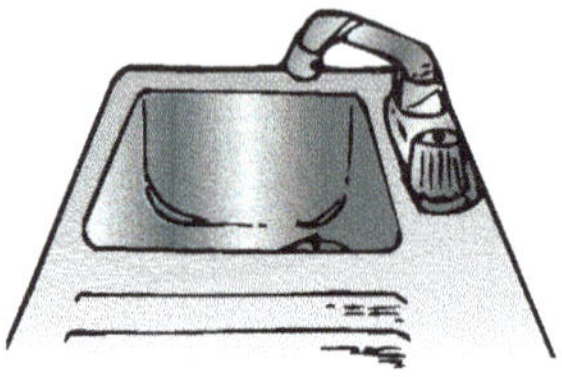

8
fi

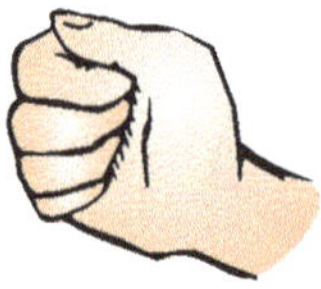

9
sku

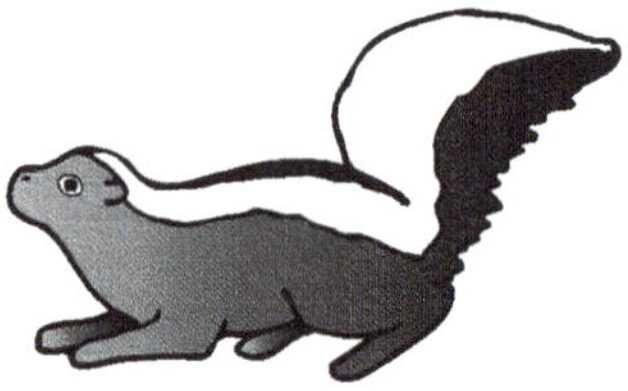

Name

Name each picture. Listen for the sounds at the end of the word.
Circle the word and print it.

© Continental Press

Read the story. Circle the word that completes each sentence. Print the missing word in each sentence.

See the nest on the ____________ .	click class cliff
The nest has sticks and ____________ in it.	brass grass gruff
It is the nest of a ____________ .	gull gust grill
The gull has ____________ wing tips.	blast black blank
There is a red spot on its ____________ .	bell blink bill

Name

Chair begins with the sound /ch/.
We print the letters ch for the sound /ch/.
Sheep begins with the sound /sh/.
We print the letters sh for the sound /sh/.

Name each picture. Print the letters it begins with – ch or sh.

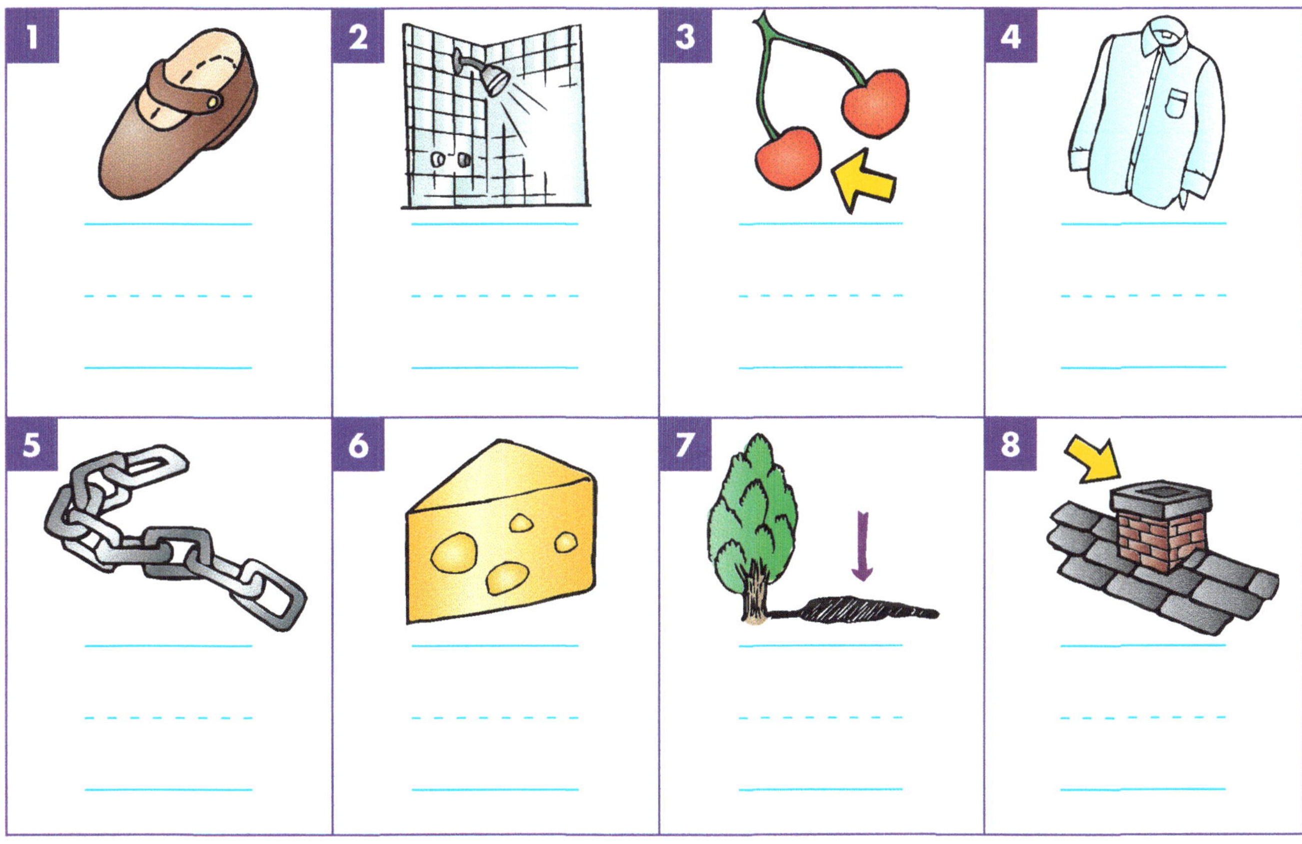

© Continental Press

Name each picture. Find the word that begins with the same sound. Circle that word and print it.

Initial consonant digraphs in words: **ch** and **sh**

Name

Thumb begins with the sound /th/.
We print the letters th for the sound /th/.
Wheel begins with the sound /wh/.
We print the letters wh for the sound /wh/.

Name each picture. Print the letters it begins with – th or wh.

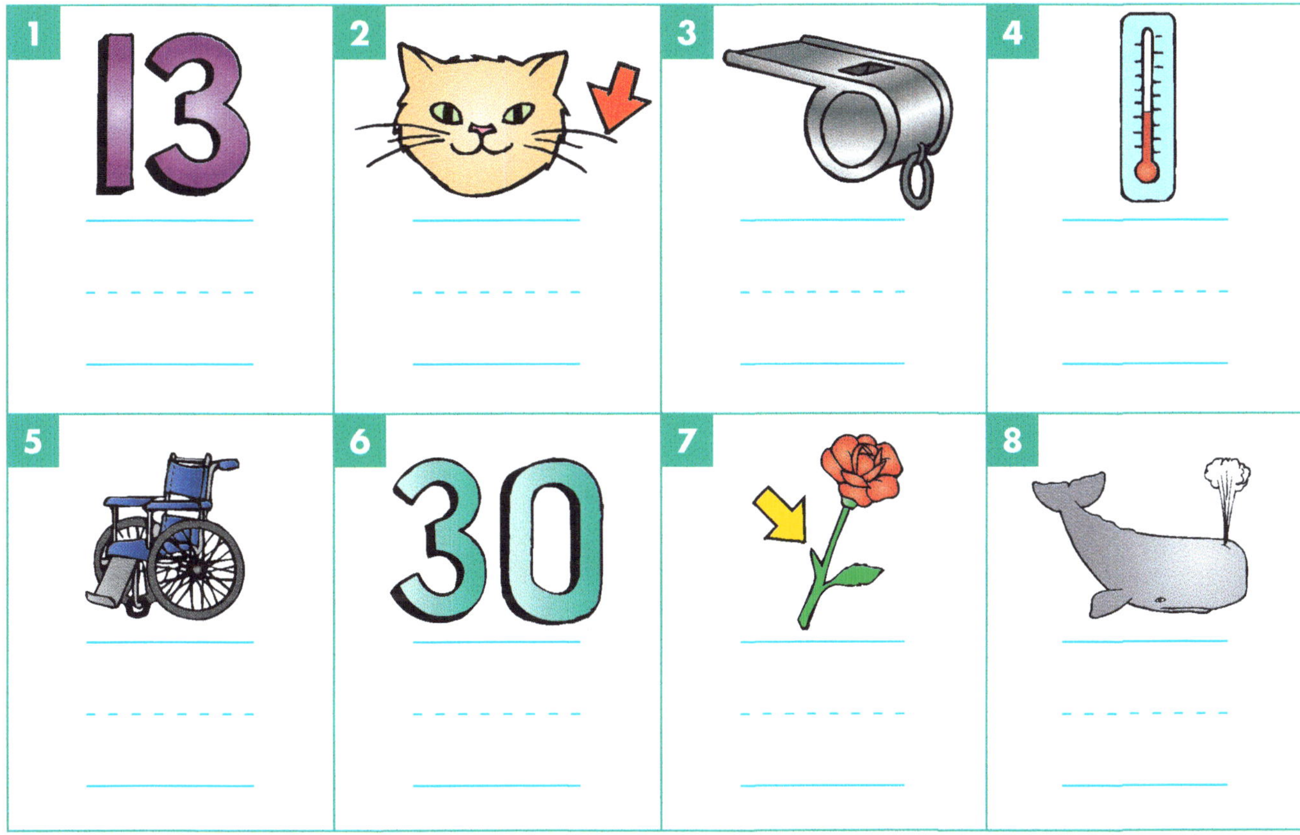

© Continental Press

Name each picture. Listen for the beginning sound.
Print the letters to complete each word.

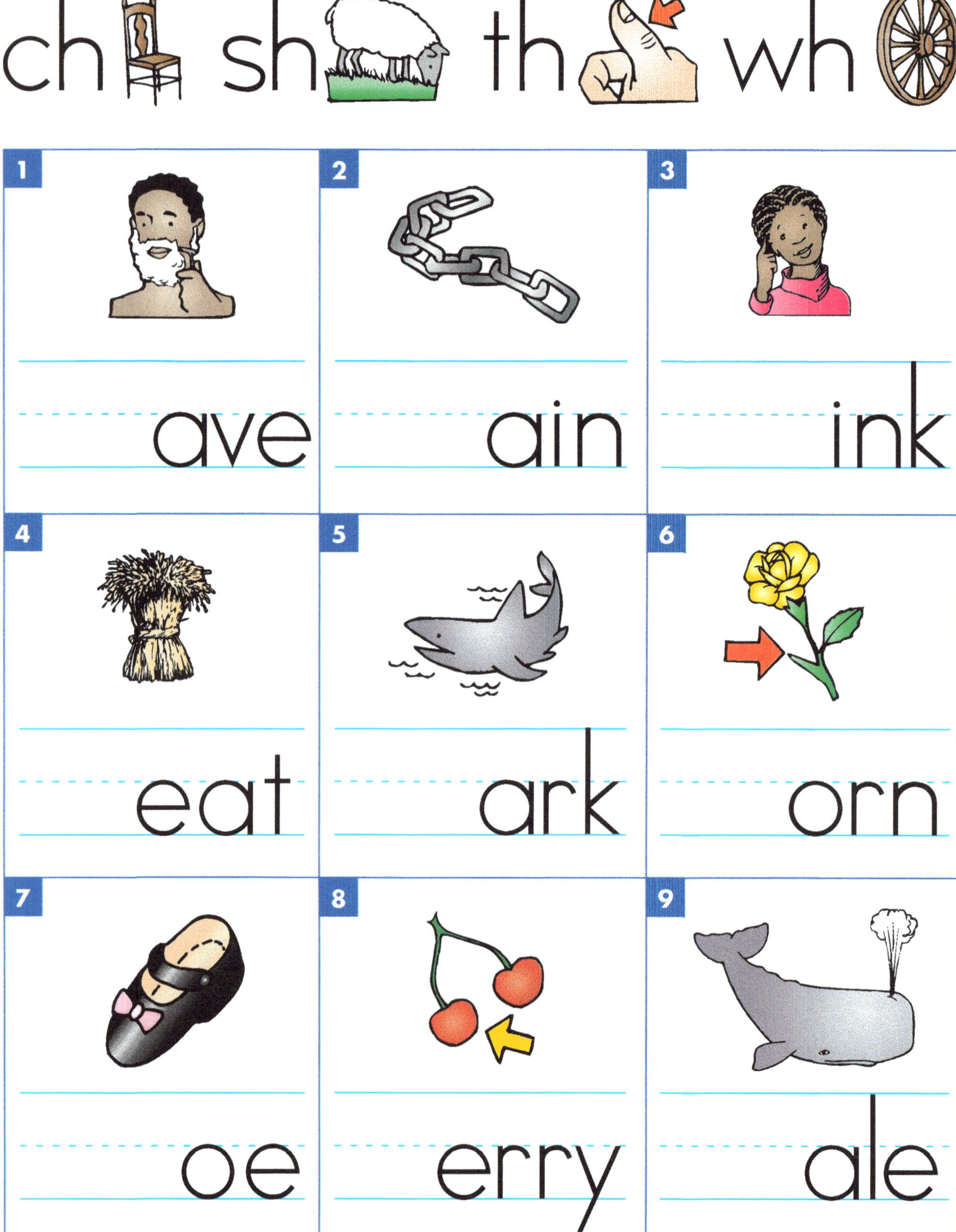

Name

Name each picture. Circle the letters for the sound at the end of the word.
Print the letters to complete the word.

brush wreath watch

© Continental Press

Read the story. Circle the word that completes each sentence. Print the missing word in each sentence.

Mom sent me to get ______ eggs.	frost fresh fish
Which eggs do you ______ will be best?	thin this think
I ______ they were not on the top shelf.	wish with whisk
I must not drop them, so I will ______ my step.	when watch which
Then I will ______ the eggs for cracks.	chest chess check

Name

To make the plural of most words, add s.
Add es to words that end in **s, ss, x, ch,** or **sh.**

cap

cap**s**

box

box**es**

Read each word. Say its plural and print it.

1 bat

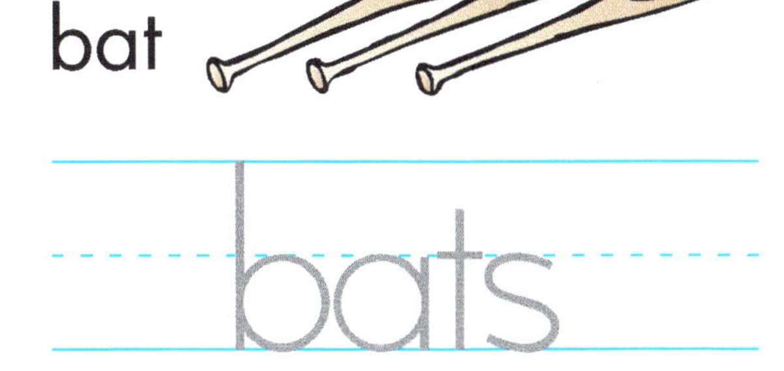

2 brush

3 dress

4 fox

5 bug

6 drum

© Continental Press

To make the plural of most words, add s.
Add es to words that end in **s, ss, x, ch,** or **sh.**

Read each word. Say its plural and print it.

1 ship

2 watch

3 duck

4 ax

5 bus

6 doll

7 dish

8 glass

Name

To make the plural of most words, add s.
Add es to words that end in **s, ss, x, ch,** or **sh.**

Read each word. Say its plural and print the plural word in the boxes. Then read down to find the hidden message. Begin reading at the ★.

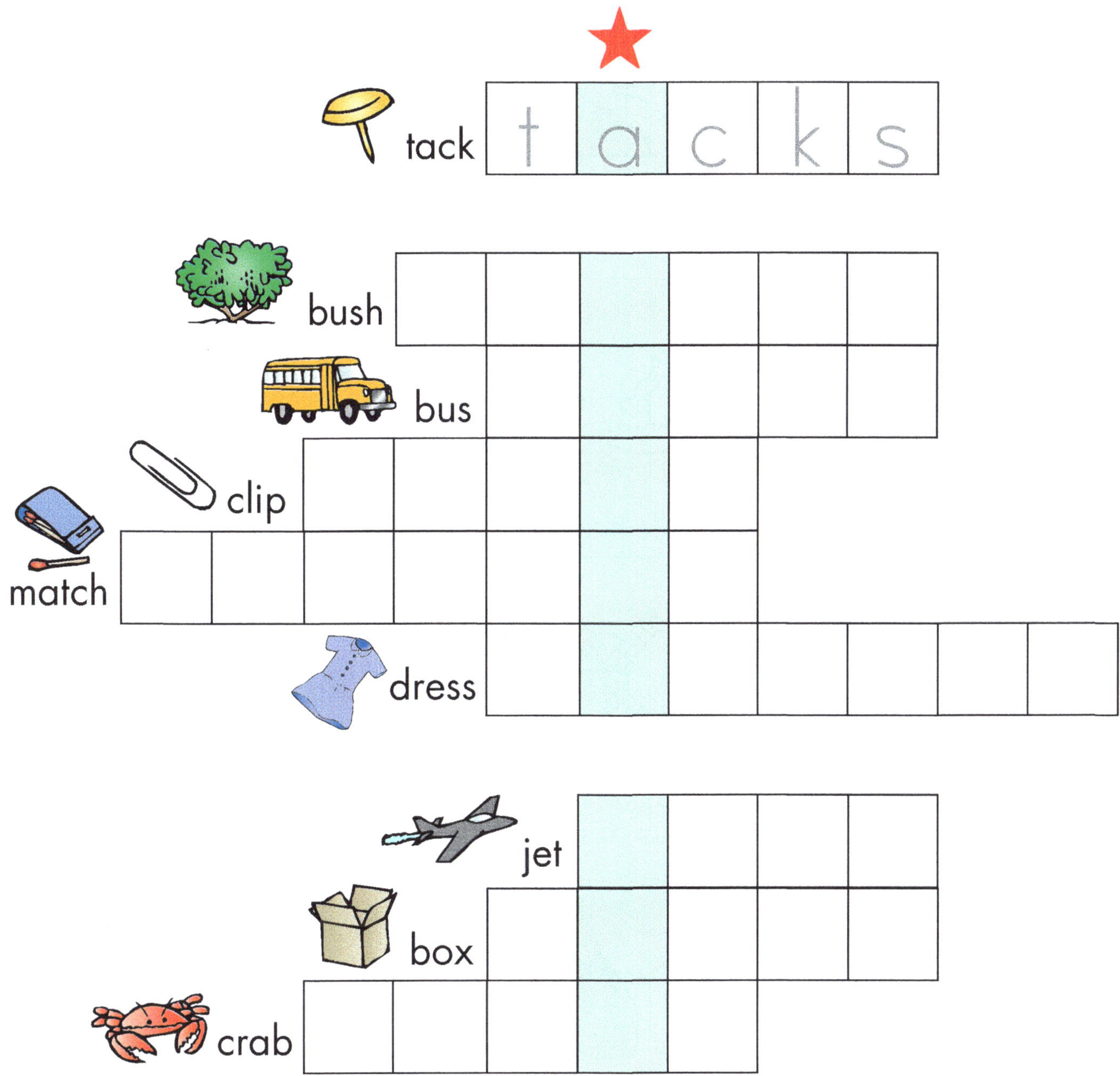

© Continental Press

Compound words are two small words put together to make one big word.

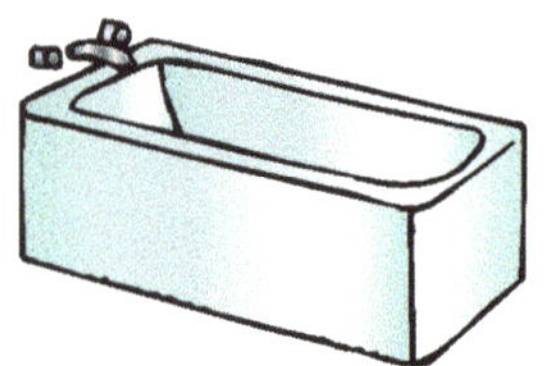

bath + tub = bathtub

Look at the pictures. Read the words.
Circle the word that goes with each picture. Print the word beside its picture.

cat • nip

sun • set

egg • shell

snap • shot

hand • bag

wind • mill

back • pack

gum • drop

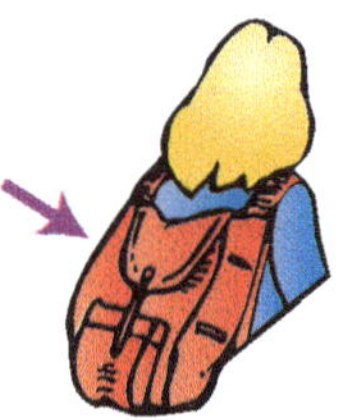

Name

Look at the pictures. Read the words.
Circle the word that goes with each picture. Print the word beside its picture.

basket

tunnel

basket

nickel

magnet

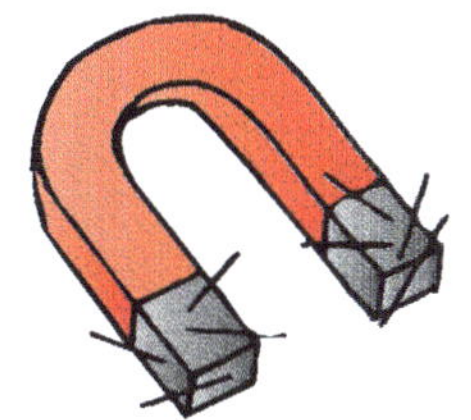

puppet

picnic

magnet

mitten

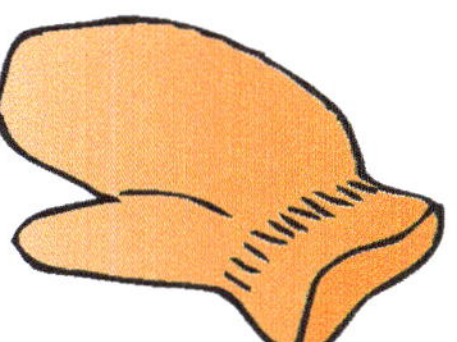

rabbit

basket

© Continental Press

Read the phrases.
Circle the phrase that goes with each picture.
Print the phrase under the picture.

a puppet for a present

a velvet rabbit

a cactus in a pot

a cotton blanket

kittens in a basket

glasses in a dishpan

frogs in a bathtub

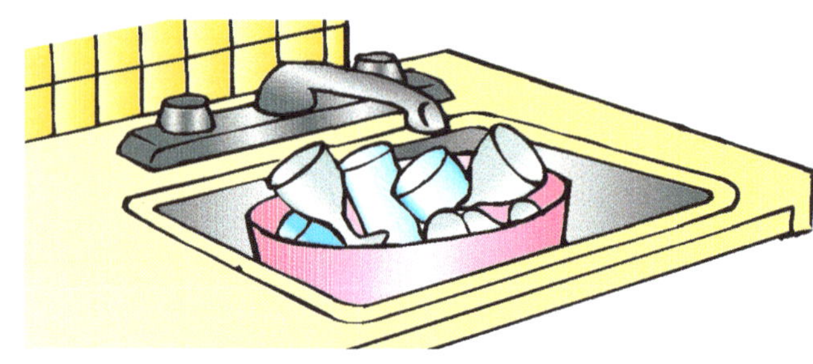

Name ______________________

Read the story. Circle the word that completes each sentence. Print the missing word in each sentence.

Grandpa is a bit ______________ . He has a big problem.	unless upset sunset
He got a ______________ , and he wants to look at it.	letter better wetter
But he ______________ find his glasses.	carrot closet cannot
"Where can they be ______________ ?" he said.	handbag hidden humbug

"They are not at the ________ of the basket."	bottom button bathtub
"My glasses are not under the ________."	rabbit blanket bracket
Then grandpa said, "I will check my ________."	picnic piglet pocket
Can you tell what will ________ next?	helmet happen hidden

Write a story about grandpa's glasses.

8 I win!

Simon Says

1

Simon says...

6 wink.

Simon says...

skip in the grass.

3

fold

cut

© Continental Press

Simon says...

2 pick up the stick.

Now blink. **7**

Simon says...

4 hop on the step.

Simon says...

clap your hands. **5**

Name

Listen to each word.
Find the word in the box and circle it.

1	2	3	4	5
eggshell handcuff handbag	catnip chestnut champ	problem puppet public	piglet picnic plastic	bedbug button humbug

6	7	8	9	10
helmet hidden hectic	dentist tennis ditch	triplet tinsel tunnel	thin skin fin	spell wells shell

11	12	13	14	15
shop chop stop	chip hill chill	miss this kiss	chick shack track	clamp damp champ

Listen to each word.
Write the letter or letters to complete the word.

1. ____uff
2. ____uff
3. ____uff
4. ____ill
5. ____ill
6. ____ill

7. ca____
8. ca____
9. ba____
10. ba____
11. mix____
12. pet____

The Swing

How do you like to go up in a swing,
Up in the air so blue?
Oh, I do think it the pleasantest thing
Ever a child can do!

Up in the air and over the wall,
Till I can see so wide,
Rivers and trees and cattle and all
Over the countryside—

Till I look down on the garden green,
Down on the roof so brown—
Up in the air I go flying again,
Up in the air and down!

Robert Louis Stevenson

Dear Family,

Our class is now learning the long vowel sounds in words like **game, bike, rode,** and **cube.** An easy way to remember long vowel sounds is that they sound like the name of the letter—**a, e, i, o,** and **u.** We will also be learning about words that have **-ed** and **-ing** endings. By now your child is probably reading and recognizing many new words.

Here are a few ways that you can help your child at home.

- When your child brings home a booklet such as the story "Simon Says," read it together. Listen as your child reads the story aloud. Then ask questions and talk about the story to be sure your child understands what was read.
- As you are riding in the car, play a guessing game. Say, "I see something that has the long **a** sound and is full of water." Give other clues (It begins like **lily.**) and let your child try to guess what it is (**lake**). Continue the game with other objects that have long vowel sounds in their names.
- Read the poem on the other side of this page aloud and talk about it. Your child will be able to read some of the words in the poem.
- You and your child might enjoy reading *Brave Norman* by Andrew Clements together on your next library visit.

Name

Listen for the long **a** sound in **game.**
The long **a** sound is like the name of the letter.

game

Name each picture.
Circle the picture if you hear the long **a** sound.

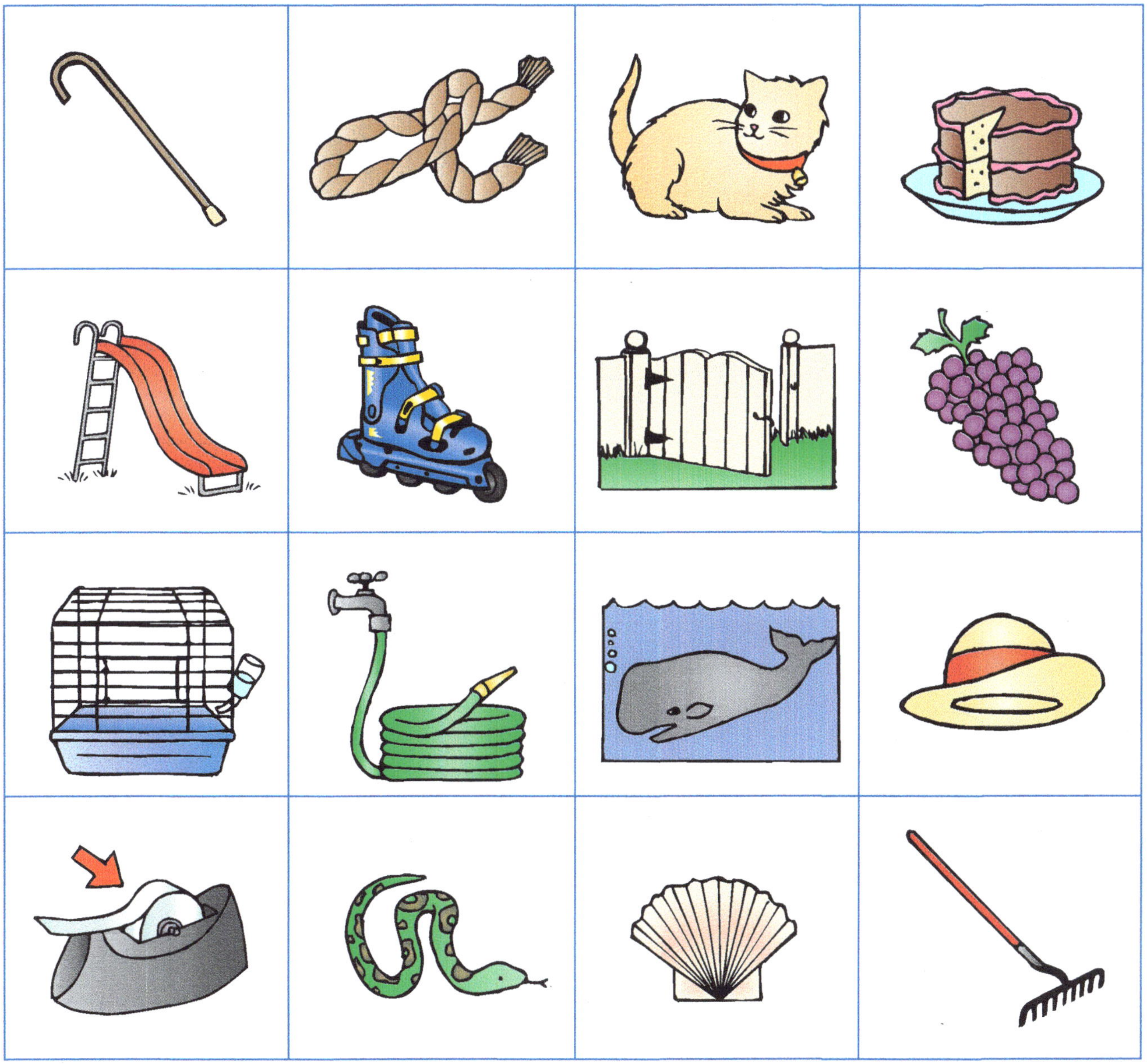

Read the words beside each picture.
Circle the word that names the picture. Print the word.

can

cane

1 cap / cape	2 mat / mate	3 hat / hate
4 man / mane	5 tap / tape	6 pan / pane
7 plan / plane	8 mad / made	9 at / ate

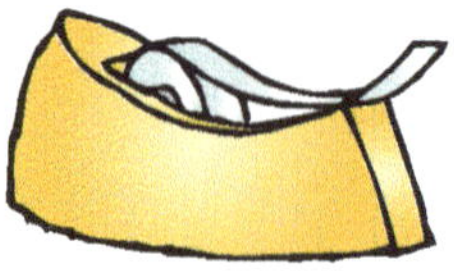

Name ______________________

Listen for the long **i** sound in **bike.**
The long **i** sound is like the name of the letter.

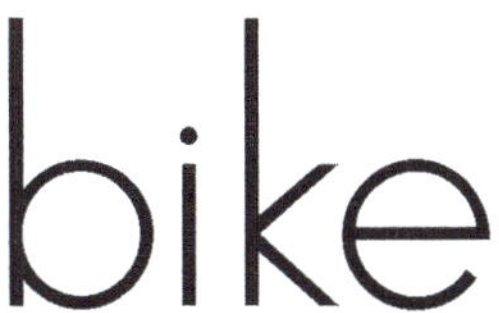

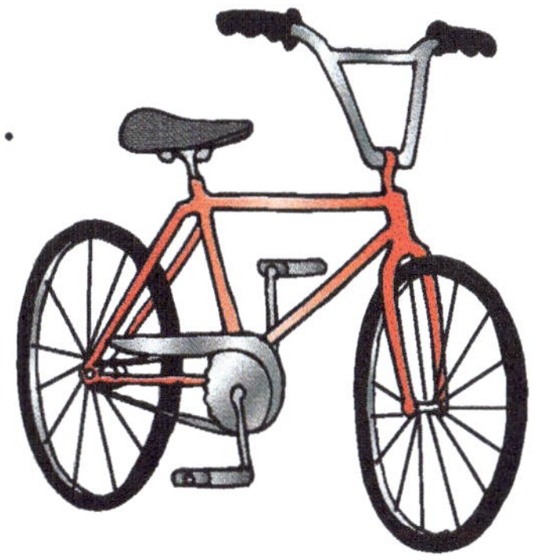

bike

Name each picture.
Circle the picture if you hear the long **i** sound.

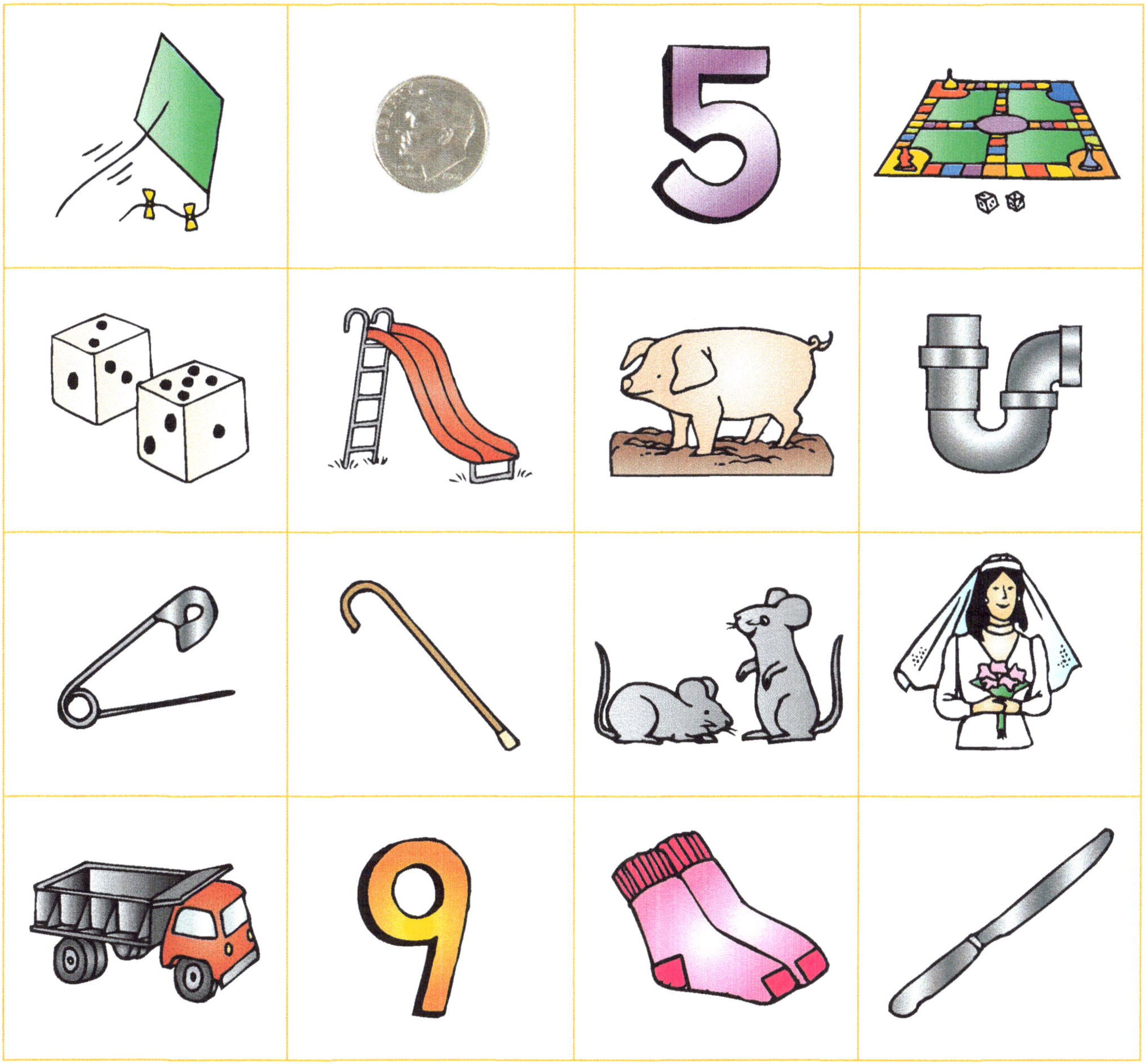

© *Continental Press*

Read the words beside each picture.
Circle the word that names the picture. Print the word.

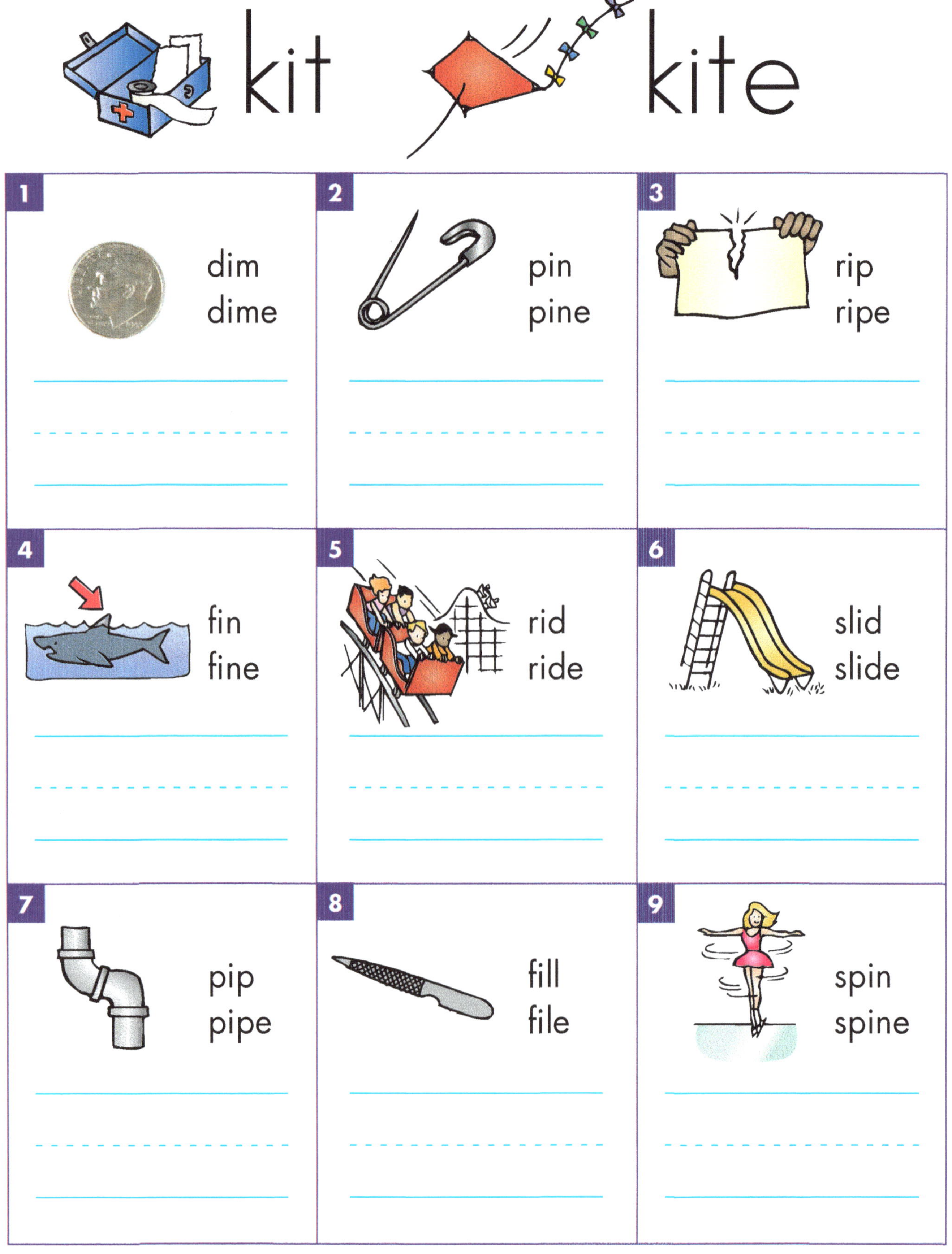

Name

Read the words beside each picture.
Choose the word that names the picture. Fill in the circle beside it.
Then print two sentences using the words that go with the pictures.

○ game
○ gate
○ tame
○ tam

○ tin
○ fire
○ tire
○ time

○ case
○ can
○ shave
○ cave

○ nine
○ nice
○ mice
○ nip

© Continental Press

Read each sentence. Circle the word that completes the sentence. Print the missing word in each sentence.

1. If I want to take a hike, then you want to ride your ______.	like mike bike
2. If I want to run a mile, then you want to rest a ______.	while smile pile
3. If I want to swim or dive, then you want to take a ______.	wide tide drive
4. If I want to slide or skate, you tell me that it is ______.	slate late gate
5. If I want to play a game, you never want to do the ______.	shame name same

Name

Listen for the long **o** sound in **globe.**
The long **o** sound is like the name of the letter.

globe

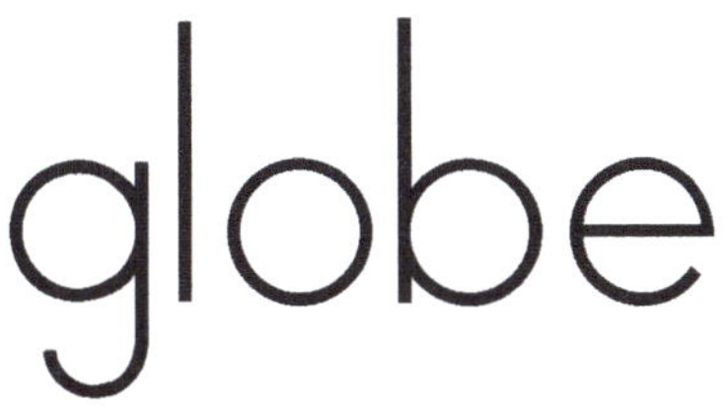

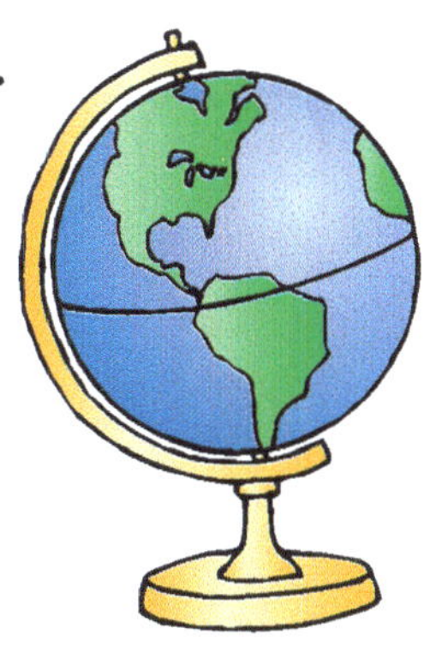

Name each picture.
Circle the picture if you hear the long **o** sound.

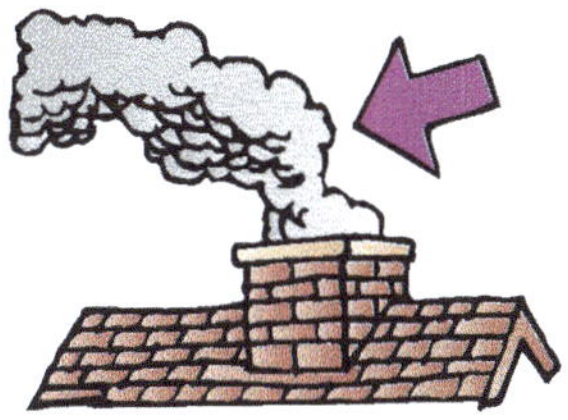
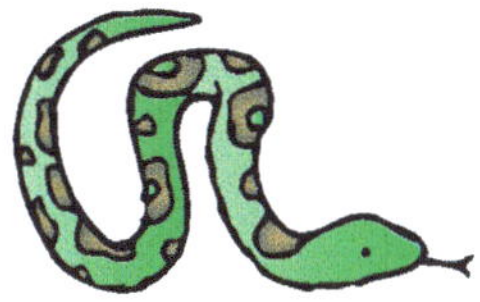
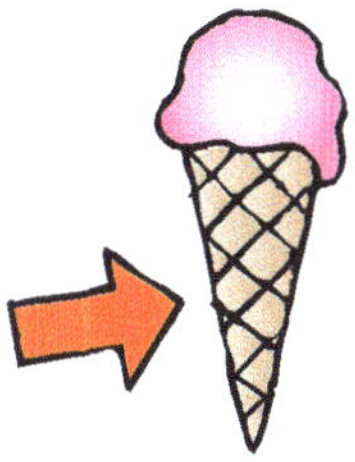
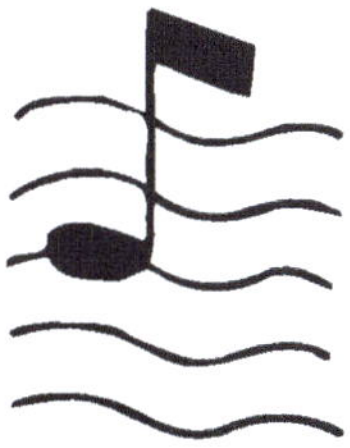
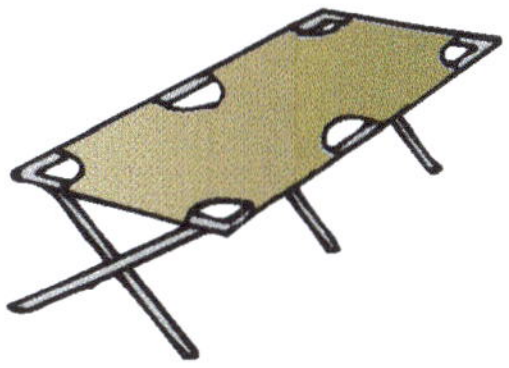
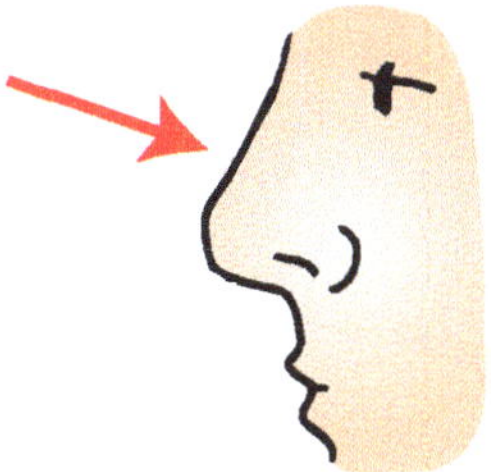
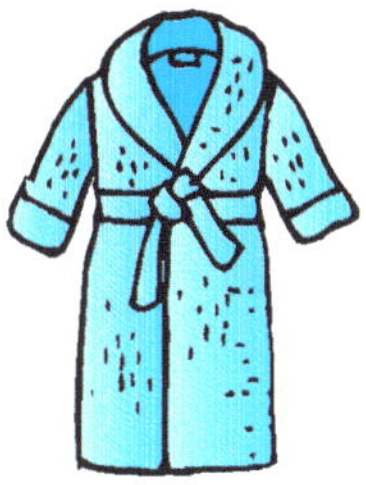
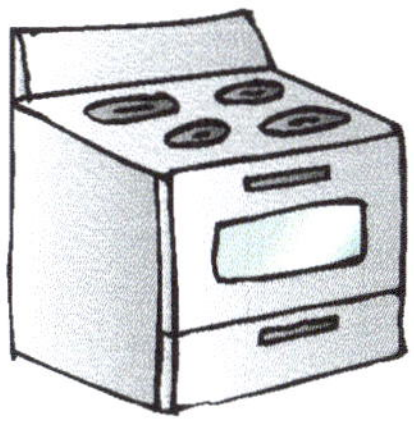
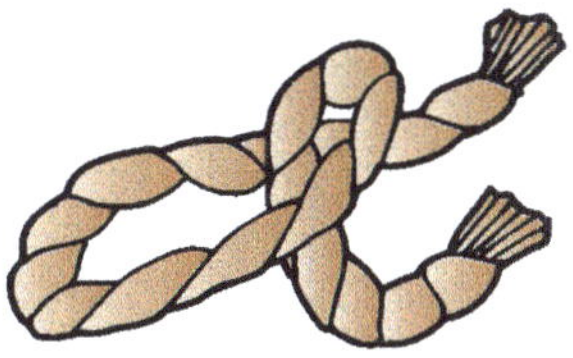
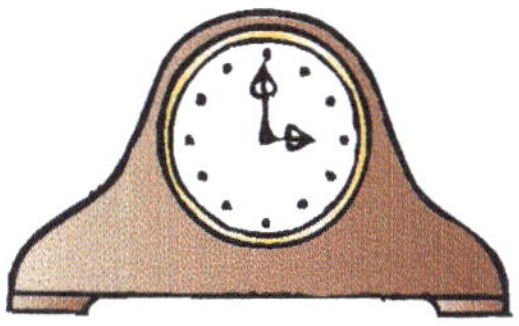
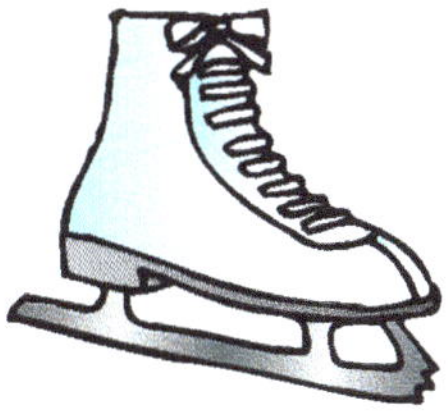
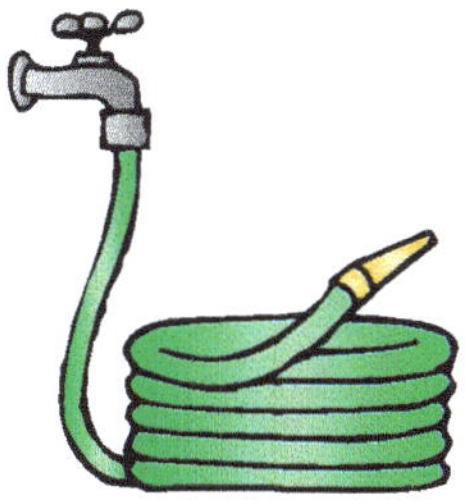
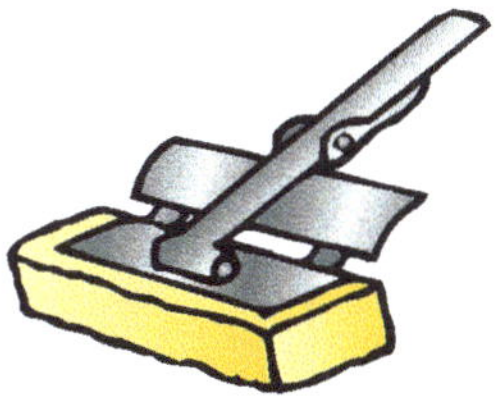
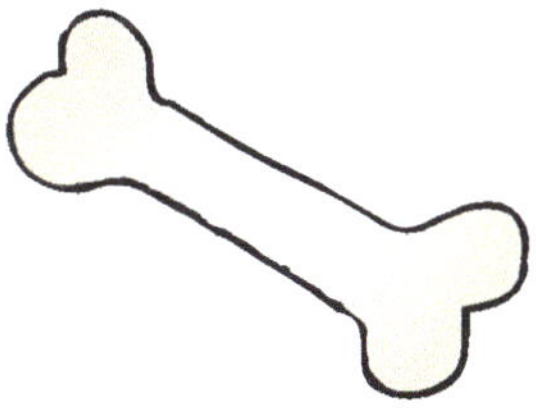
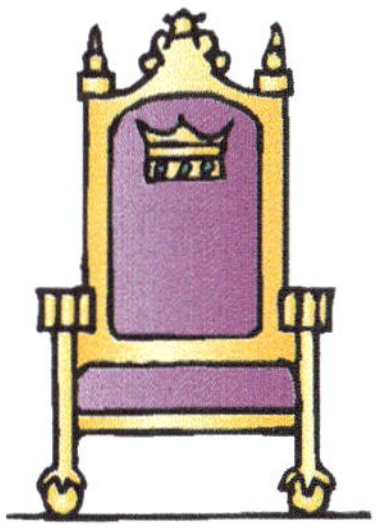

© Continental Press

Listen for the long **u** sound in **mule.**
The long **u** sound is like the name of the letter.

mule

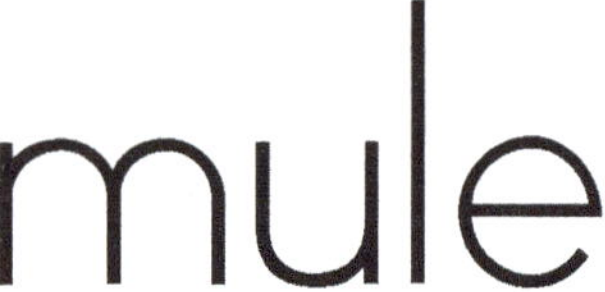

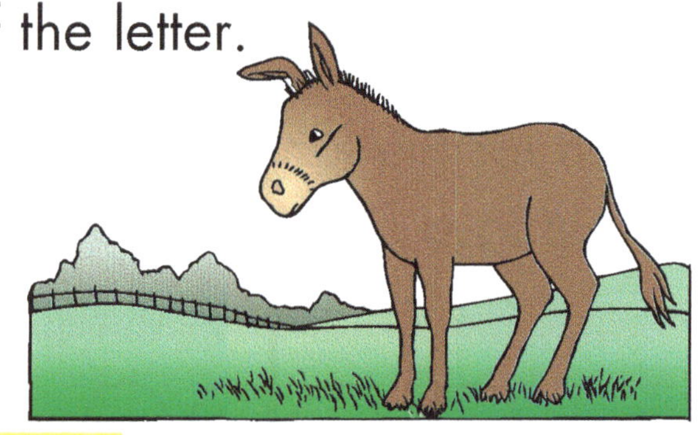

Name each picture.
Circle the picture if you hear the long **u** sound.

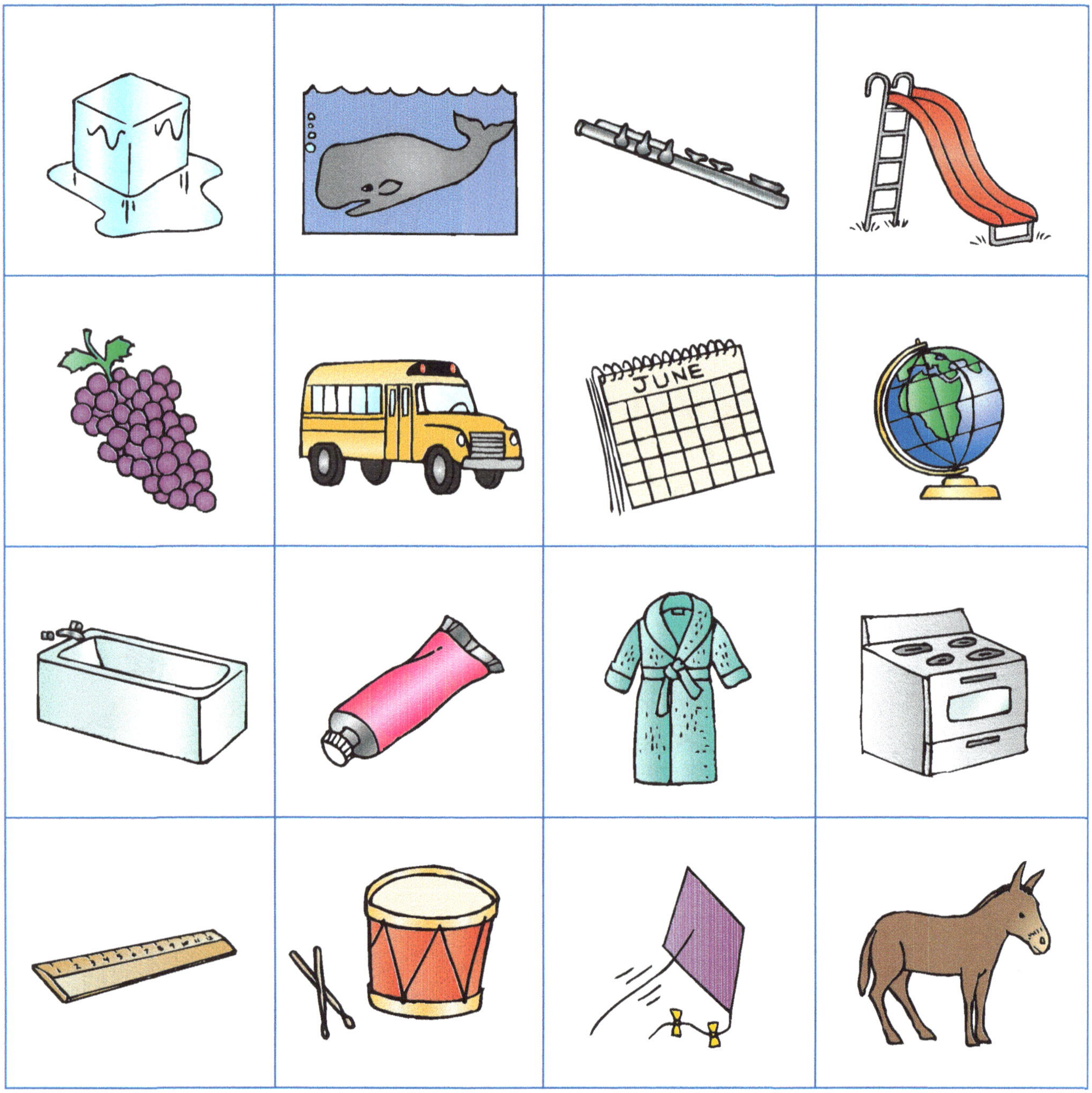

Name

Read the words beside each picture.
Circle the word that names the picture. Print the word.

 tot

 tote

 cub

 cube

1
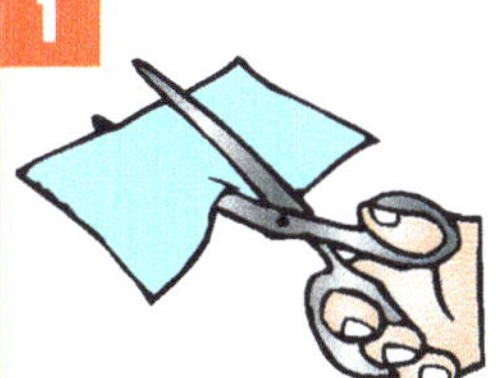
cut
cute

2

not
note

3

tub
tube

4

mop
mope

5

cod
code

6

glob
globe

7

rob
robe

8

hug
huge

9

mull
mule

© Continental Press

Read the words beside each picture.
Choose the word that names the picture. Fill in the circle beside it.
Then print two sentences using the words that go with the pictures.

- ○ mile
- ○ mill
- ○ rule
- ○ mule

- ○ can
- ○ cone
- ○ cane
- ○ bone

- ○ hope
- ○ hop
- ○ rope
- ○ ripe

- ○ cube
- ○ tribe
- ○ tube
- ○ tub

Name ____________________

Read the story. Circle the word that completes each sentence. Print the missing word in each sentence.

Luke and I ate at ____________ o'clock.	fix five hive
Then we rode our bikes to the ____________.	gas game stove
I made a hit and stole a ____________.	base bass bat
Luke hit a ____________ run. He had a big smile on his face.	hose hill home
We made two runs for our ____________. I think that we will win this game!	shade wide side

© Continental Press

Read the story. Circle the word that completes each sentence. Print the missing word in each sentence.

Kate ______ her bike to the pet shop. She went inside to get a pet.	rod rode code
She saw ______ mice, kittens, fish, and dogs.	cute flute cut
Then she saw a ______ rabbit in a big cage.	while white which
The rabbit ______ from her hand and made Kate smile.	gate at ate
Kate will take the rabbit ______ with her. It will make a nice pet.	hope home hum

Name ______________________________

base word	endings
pack	+ing
pack	+ed

Jack is packing his bag.

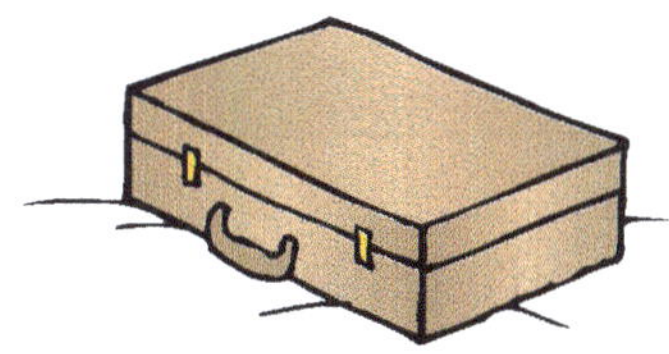

Jill packed her bag last night.

Draw a line from each word to the correct picture.

dressed
dressing

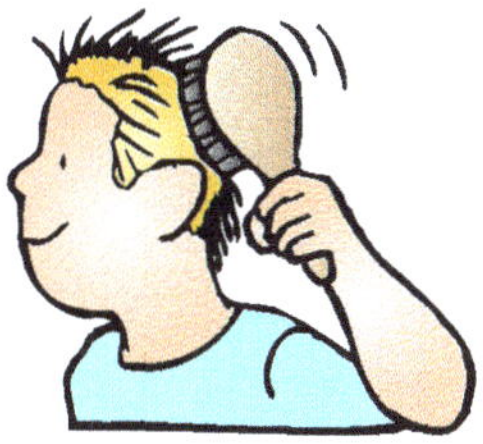

brushed
brushing

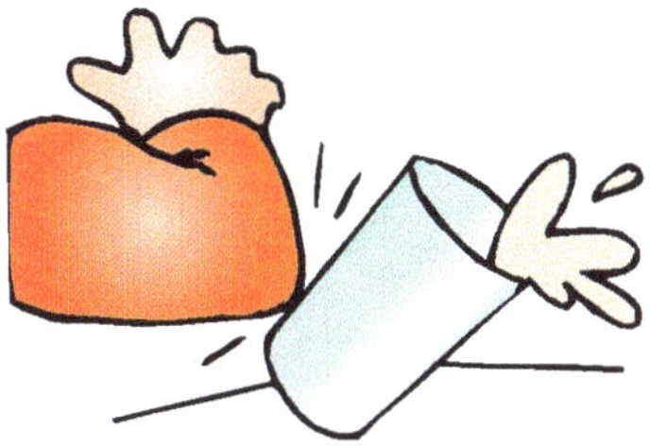

spilled
spilling

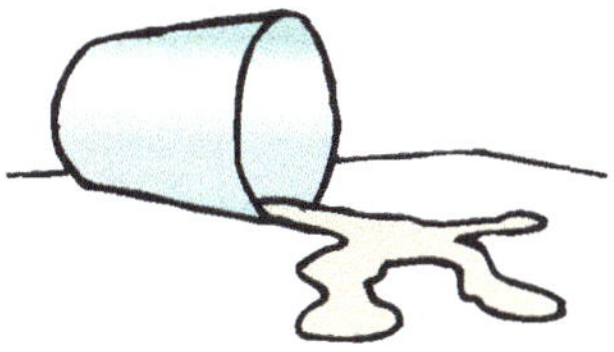

planted
planting

© Continental Press

base word	endings
rak~~e~~	+ing
rak~~e~~	+ed

Mia is raking her yard.

Pia raked her yard last night.

Draw a line from each word to the correct picture.

shaved
shaving

baked
baking

skated
skating

tamed
taming

Name ______________________

Read the story. Circle the word that completes each sentence. Print the missing word in each sentence.

One day Shane was ____________ home on Pine Lane.	diving driving drive
He saw a hen and chicks ____________ still in the lane.	stand standing stands
The hen was ____________ in the mud.	pecking pecked pecks
Shane put the ____________ on and came to a stop.	braked braking brakes

© Continental Press

He got out and ______ up the hen. Then he set her in the grass.	picking pick picked
The chicks ______ across the lane to get to the hen.	dashed dashing dashes
Shane ______ to the drivers who were in back of his truck.	wave waving waved
All the drivers were ______ as they went by.	smiled smiling smiles

Write a story about something you saw while you were riding.

fold

1

Five children are taking a ride. 3

6 Niles lets James ride his bike.
Rosa and Kate make up a game.

8 What do you like to do in the summer?

© Continental Press

2 What do these children like to do in summer?

The gate is closing.
Time to go home. **7**

4 Hope is going down the slide.
June is swinging on a rope.

Mike is diving in the lake.
Paco sits in an inner tube. **5**

Name ______________________

Listen to each word.
Find the word in the box and circle it.

1	2	3	4	5
fat fate fad fade	mill mile hid hide	cod code cube cure	smock smoke smile mile	lime lame slim slime

6	7	8	9	10
mill mile mull mule	fuss fuse fill file	bad bade back bake	shape shin shine shade	rob robe rip ripe

11	12	13	14	15
strip stripe scare score	not note hat hate	hug huge wag wage	spit spite spin spine	sham shame shack shake

© Continental Press

Read all the words in each box.
Then circle the base word for each underlined word.

1	2	3	4	5
spelled	click	smile	us	yet
spell	kicked	smell	use	yelled
shell	kick	smiled	used	yell
spelling	kicking	smiling	using	yelling

6	7	8	9	10
watch	clock	hop	mint	filled
watched	clicking	hope	mixed	filed
watching	clicked	hoping	mix	filing
wash	click	hoped	mixing	file

11	12	13	14	15
drilling	crush	hike	small	wing
doll	crash	hiked	smelling	winked
drill	crashing	hiking	smelled	wink
drilled	crashed	hiker	smell	winking

Sun After Rain

Rain, rain,
went away.
Sun came out
with pipe of clay,
blew a bubble
whole-world-wide,
stuck a rainbow
on one side.

Norma Farber

Dear Family,

Rainy days, sunny days, any day is a good day to read a book! During the school year, we learned sounds for all the letters of the alphabet. Then we blended the sounds together to make words and to read sentences. Now we are learning about some words with long vowel sounds that are spelled in different ways (tr**ay**, n**ai**l; l**ea**f, str**ee**t; b**oa**t). Your child has made progress in reading, writing, and spelling skills during this school year.

At the close of this school year and during the summer, here are a few ways that you can help your child at home.

- Together choose favorite books to reread, including the take-home stories from this book. Reading stories again and again helps children develop fluency and understanding.
- Your child can practice writing words in new ways. A laminated wipe-off board is always fun to write on. Your child might type words using a computer keyboard and write short letters to friends or relatives.
- Read the poem on the other side of this page aloud. Talk about things you can do on sunny days and rainy days. Encourage your child to read the poem with you and tell you the words that rhyme.
- Don't forget to visit the library over the summer. There are many series of early readers you can share with your child. Here are just three to look for: *I Can Read Books* from HarperCollins, *Steps Into Reading* from Random House and *Brand New Readers* from Candlewick Press.

Name ______________________________

The letters **ai** and **ay** stand for the long **a** sound.

 **nail**

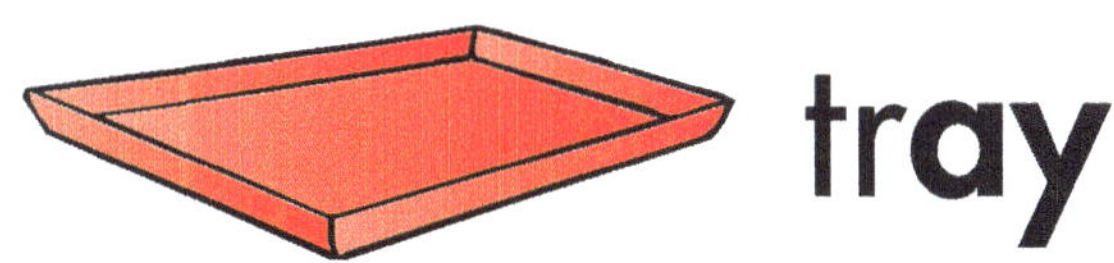 **tray**

Look at each picture. Read the phrase next to it. Choose a word to complete the phrase. Fill in the circle beside it. Print the word in the phrase.

1	a thick ______________	○ chain ○ pain ○ brain
2	a hot ______________	○ stay ○ may ○ day
3	five ______________	○ snails ○ nails ○ tails
4	______________ in the sand	○ gray ○ play ○ pay
5	______________ for the bus	○ wait ○ bait ○ trait

© Continental Press

Read the words beside each picture.
Circle the word that names the picture. Print the word.

1

$$\begin{array}{r} 2 \\ +3 \\ \hline 5 \end{array}$$

add
aid

2

ran
rain

3

trap
tray

4

pal
pail

5

pan
pain

6

pant
paint

7

van
vain

8

grab
gray

9

bat
bait

Name ______________________________

The letters **oa** stand for the long **o** sound.

boat

Look at each picture. Read the phrase next to it. Choose a word to complete the phrase. Fill in the circle beside it. Print the word in the phrase.

1	a jumping ______	○ load ○ toad ○ road
2	a big ______	○ boat ○ goat ○ coat
3	hot ______	○ toast ○ roast ○ coast
4	______ in the lake	○ boat ○ float ○ coat
5	______ in the tub	○ soak ○ oak ○ cloak

© Continental Press

Read the words beside each picture.
Circle the word that names the picture. Print the word.

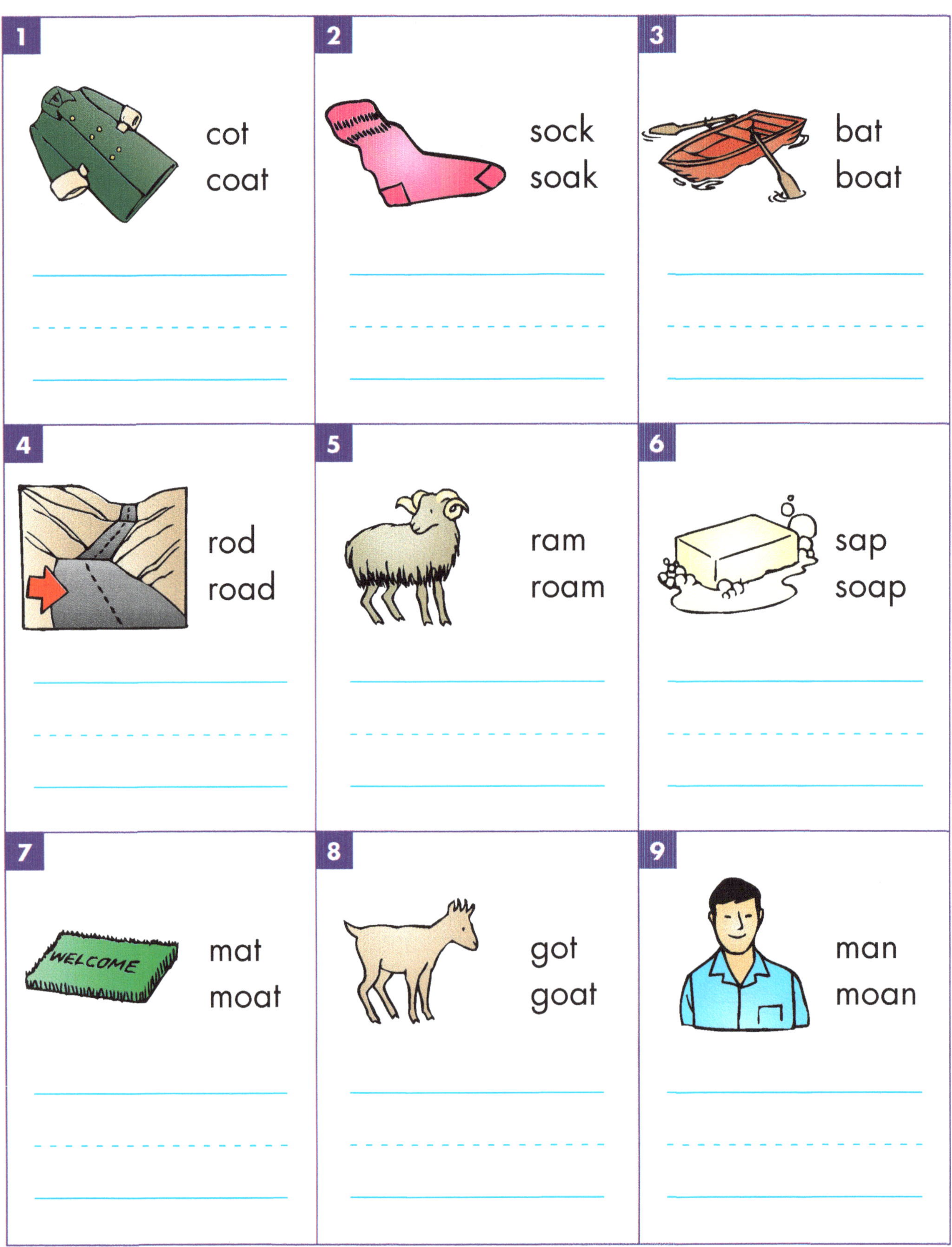

Name

The letters **ee** stand for the long **e** sound.

queen

Look at each picture. Read the phrase next to it. Choose a word to complete the phrase. Fill in the circle beside it. Print the word in the phrase.

1	a black ______	○ sweep ○ sleep ○ sheep
2	a wagon ______	○ wheel ○ feel ○ peel
3	planting ______	○ bleeds ○ seeds ○ needs
4	______ buns	○ feet ○ meet ○ sweet
5	______ in the box	○ peek ○ cheek ○ week

© Continental Press

Read the words beside each picture.
Circle the word that names the picture. Print the word.

Name ______________________

The letters **ea** also stand for the long **e** sound.

Look at each picture. Read the phrase next to it. Choose a word to complete the phrase. Fill in the circle beside it. Print the word in the phrase.

1	the best ______	○ cream ○ steam ○ team
2	a big ______	○ leak ○ beak ○ sneak
3	______ on a rock	○ heal ○ steal ○ seal
4	______ a page	○ read ○ bead ○ lead
5	______ the drum	○ heat ○ seat ○ beat

© Continental Press

Read the words beside each picture.
Circle the word that names the picture. Print the word.

Name ______________________

Read the letter Jeff sent home from camp. Circle the word that completes each sentence. Print the missing word in each sentence.

Dear Mom and Dad,	
We have had lots of ______________ , but I like it here just the same.	ran rain read
We get up at six o'clock. They do not let us ______________ late.	green leap sleep
We do crafts, hike, swim, and ______________ on the lake.	sail seal steep
We had a ______________ race yesterday. My team won!	bean boat beet

© Continental Press

The prize was ice ______, a big dish for all of us.	cream crime cram
Today we hiked five miles and had lunch near a big ______ tree.	soak sock oak
The hike was fun, but my ______ are still sore.	feed faint feet
Now it is time to ______ dinner. I will see you next Sunday. Love, Jeff	cheek eat pail

Write another letter from Jeff or from you.

Name

The letter **y** at the end of a one-syllable word often stands for the **long i** sound.

y = i
fl**y**

The letter **y** at the end of a word with more than one syllable often stands for the **long e** sound.

y = e
penn**y**

Read the picture names.
Under **fly,** print the words that have the **long i** sound.
Under **penny,** print the words that have the **long e** sound at the end.

fl**y**

penn**y**

© *Continental Press*

Read each sentence. Circle the words that complete each sentence. Print the words in the sentence.

1. On a ________________, fly your kite.	windy day silly try
2. Did you hear the ________________?	muddy daisy puppy cry
3. A ________________ is hiding in the grass.	shy bunny sly buggy
4. The ________________ landed on my nose.	funny sky ugly fly
5. Today is a ________________.	runny spy sunny day

Name

A contraction is a short way to write two words as one.
An apostrophe (’) shows where letters are left out.

I am = **I’m**	she is = **she’s**	we are = **we’re**
I will = **I’ll**	he is = **he’s**	you are = **you’re**
	it is = **it’s**	they are = **they’re**

Read the words on the flowers. Color each flower part that shows a contraction that stands for the two words below it.

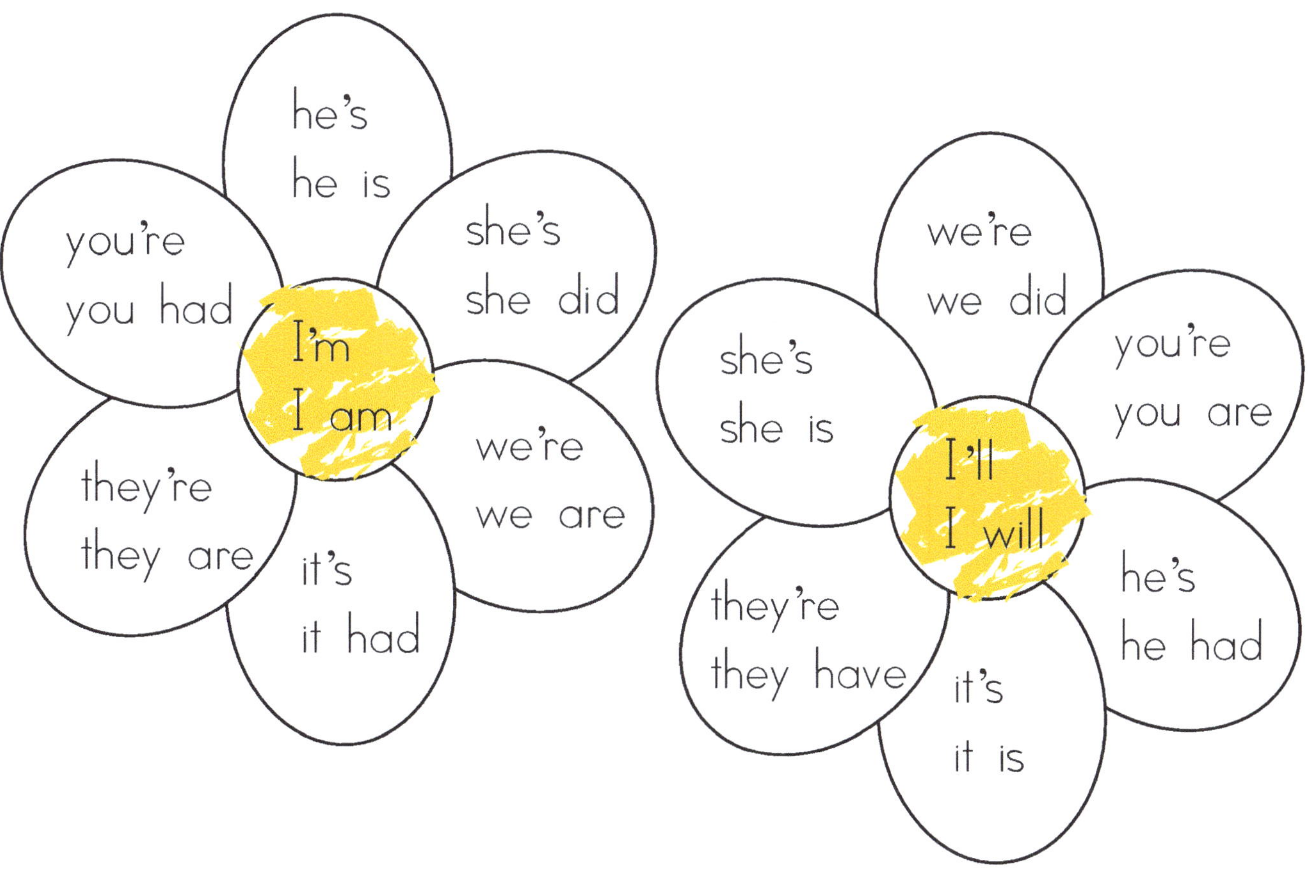

© Continental Press

Many contractions can be made with **not.**
The box below shows you some of them.

is not = **isn't**	cannot = **can't**	have not = **haven't**
are not = **aren't**	do not = **don't**	has not = **hasn't**
was not = **wasn't**	did not = **didn't**	had not = **hadn't**
were not = **weren't**	does not = **doesn't**	

Read the words in each box.
Print the contraction that stands for the words.

1 are not aren't	**2** has not	**3** were not
4 does not	**5** is not	**6** was not
7 have not	**8** did not	**9** cannot
10 do not	**11** are not	**12** had not

Name ______________________

Read the story. Circle the contraction that stands for the underlined words.

Roxy is my puppy. She <u>was not</u> very clean.	weren't wasn't we're
Roxy <u>had not</u> had a bath lately. Her coat was all muddy.	hadn't haven't aren't
But Roxy <u>does not</u> like baths. She ran away.	hasn't doesn't aren't
"I <u>cannot</u> catch Roxy," I said to Dad.	didn't isn't can't

© Continental Press

"I am going to need some help." So Dad helped me catch Roxy.	I'm I'll it's
Then Dad got the hose. Now we are both giving Roxy a bath.	you're we're they're
Roxy is not a muddy puppy any more. But we're all soapy and wet!	can't isn't didn't
Dad thinks it is funny. What a way to spend a sunny day!	he's I'm it's

Write a story about your pet. The story doesn't have to be true.

© Continental Press

8 Hector will make his own book.
It will be about trucks.

fold

1

6 Kaley wants a book with games.
She is learning to play chess.

Amy is looking for a picture book.
She likes books about bugs. 3

2 Mrs. Ray's class is going
to the library today.

Joan has a chapter book.
It is about a girl like her. **7**

4 Mike likes to read story books.
He has found a good one.

Dean finds a book about animals.
He has a new puppy. **5**

Name

Listen to each word.
Find the word in the box and circle it.

1	2	3	4	5
pad	pal	plan	fed	raid
paid	pail	plain	feed	reed
dad	peel	pan	fell	road
deed	peek	pain	foal	ride
6	**7**	**8**	**9**	**10**
off	cot	see	say	sped
oak	coat	set	sail	speed
am	take	wee	same	spade
aim	teak	wet	sty	span
11	**12**	**13**	**14**	**15**
fleck	free	got	my	clock
flea	fret	goat	mail	cloak
peck	bee	cot	meal	clean
pea	bet	coat	may	clan

In each box, circle the words that stand for the underlined contraction.

1 <u>we're</u> they are we are we will	**2** <u>aren't</u> do not were not are not	**3** <u>he's</u> she is he is he will
4 <u>I'm</u> I am I will I have	**5** <u>haven't</u> has not have not will have	**6** <u>you're</u> you are you will you have
7 <u>doesn't</u> do not does not did not	**8** <u>they're</u> they have they will they are	**9** <u>can't</u> cannot will not I can

Read the word in each box. Then circle the letter that stands for the long vowel sound you hear at the end of the word.

10 spy a e i	**11** play a e i	**12** why a e i
13 sandy a e i	**14** grumpy a e i	**15** spray a e i